"This pilgrim's progress of o[...]
growth has the ring of tru[...]
wisdom that can come only from difficult clinical experience
approached with relentless inquiry and ruthless honesty. Clearly knowing our several theories, Sedlak transcends their limits, staying ever true
to the anguished uncertainties of clinical actuality. Compelling to read,
this beautifully written report of one analyst's struggles was, for me,
emotionally evocative and educationally enlightening. It is a compelling
master class in the perplexity of analytic exploration, where each journey is original and unique."
— **Warren S. Poland**, Sigourney Awardee 2009, Author,
Intimacy and Separateness in Psychoanalysis

"Vic Sedlak is much admired as a psychoanalyst who can sustain
an independent point of view and is not afraid to speak his mind.
Here he examines the role of the analyst's reactions and responses
in the psychoanalytic session. He covers a wide field but for me he
is particularly convincing when he describes how the analyst's
responsiveness is especially affected by his capacity to accept the
emergence of hatred, hostility and destructiveness in his patient
and also in himself. His arguments and the vivid clinical material
make for fascinating reading that all those working in the mental
health field will find valuable and stimulating."
— **John Steiner**, Training and Supervising Psychoanalyst,
Distinguished Fellow, British Psychoanalytical Society

"Anyone who is interested in understanding the unconscious
dynamics in the therapist/patient relationship will be rewarded by
reading Vic Sedlak's accessible and insightful study of the 'glancing'
thought; the thought that the clinician resists knowing without
knowing he or she is avoiding it. Sedlak, a highly respected and
experienced psychoanalyst, writes openly and honestly about the
role his super-ego and ego ideal play in supporting or impeding his
efforts to recognise and understand the glancing thought in his ongoing clinical practice and supervision."
— **Donald Campbell**, Training and Supervising Analyst,
Distinguished Fellow and past President,
British Psychoanalytic Society

The Psychoanalyst's Superegos, Ego Ideals and Blind Spots

Psychotherapists and psychoanalysts enter an emotional relationship when they treat a patient; no matter how experienced they may be, their personalities inform but also limit their ability to recognise and give thought to what happens in the consulting room. *The Psychoanalyst's Superegos, Ego Ideals and Blind Spots* investigates the nature of these constrictions on the clinician's sensitivity.

Vic Sedlak examines clinicians' fear of a superego which threatens to become censorious of themselves or their patient and their need to aspire to standards demanded by their ego ideals. These dynamic forces are considered in relation to treatments which fail, to supervision and to recent innovations in psychoanalytic technique. The difficulty of giving thought to hostility is particularly stressed.

Richly illustrated with clinical material, this book will enable practitioners to recognise the unconscious forces which militate against their clinical effectiveness.

Vic Sedlak is a Training and Supervising Psychoanalyst of the British Psychoanalytical Society in private practice in the North of England.

THE NEW LIBRARY OF PSYCHOANALYSIS
General Editor: Alessandra Lemma

The New Library of Psychoanalysis was launched in 1987 in association with the Institute of Psychoanalysis, London. It took over from the International Psychoanalytical Library which published many of the early translations of the works of Freud and the writings of most of the leading British and Continental psychoanalysts.

The purpose of the New Library of Psychoanalysis is to facilitate a greater and more widespread appreciation of psychoanalysis and to provide a forum for increasing mutual understanding between psychoanalysts and those working in other disciplines such as the social sciences, medicine, philosophy, history, linguistics, literature and the arts. It aims to represent different trends both in British psychoanalysis and in psychoanalysis generally. The New Library of Psychoanalysis is well placed to make available to the English-speaking world psychoanalytic writings from other European countries and to increase the interchange of ideas between British and American psychoanalysts. Through the "Teaching" series, the New Library of Psychoanalysis now also publishes books that provide comprehensive, yet accessible, overviews of selected subject areas aimed at those studying psychoanalysis and related fields such as the social sciences, philosophy, literature and the arts.

The Institute, together with the British Psychoanalytical Society, runs a low-fee psychoanalytic clinic, organises lectures and scientific events concerned with psychoanalysis and publishes the *International Journal of Psychoanalysis*. It runs a training course in psychoanalysis which leads to membership of the International Psychoanalytical Association – the body which preserves internationally agreed standards of training, of professional entry, and of professional ethics and practice for psychoanalysis as initiated and developed by Sigmund Freud. Distinguished members of the Institute have included Michael Balint, Wilfred Bion, Ronald Fairbairn, Anna Freud, Ernest Jones, Melanie Klein, John Rickman and Donald Winnicott.

Previous general editors have included David Tuckett, who played a very active role in the establishment of the New Library. He was followed as general editor by Elizabeth Bott Spillius, who was in turn followed by Susan Budd and then by Dana Birksted-Breen. Current members of the Advisory Board include Giovanna Di Ceglie, Liz Allison, Anne Patterson, Josh Cohen and Daniel Pick.

Previous members of the Advisory Board include Christopher Bollas, Ronald Britton, Catalina Bronstein, Donald Campbell, Rosemary Davies, Sara Flanders, Stephen Grosz, John Keene, Eglé Laufer, Alessandra Lemma, Juliet Mitchell, Michael Parsons, Rosine Jozef Perelberg, Richard Rusbridger, Mary Target and David Taylor.

For a full list of all the titles in the New Library of Psychoanalysis main series as well as both the New Library of Psychoanalysis "Teaching" and "Beyond the Couch" subseries, please visit the Routledge website.

THE NEW LIBRARY OF PSYCHOANALYSIS

General Editor: Alessandra Lemma

The Psychoanalyst's Superegos, Ego Ideals and Blind Spots

The Emotional Development of the Clinician

Vic Sedlak

Routledge
Taylor & Francis Group

LONDON AND NEW YORK

First published 2019
by Routledge
2 Park Square, Milton Park, Abingdon, Oxon OX14 4RN

and by Routledge
52 Vanderbilt Avenue, New York, NY 10017

Routledge is an imprint of the Taylor & Francis Group, an informa business

British Library Cataloguing-in-Publication Data
A catalogue record for this book is available from the British Library

Library of Congress Cataloging-in-Publication Data
Names: Sedlak, Vic, 1950- author.
Title: The psychoanalyst's superegos, ego ideals and blind spots :
the emotional development of the clinician / Vic Sedlak.
Description: New York : Routledge, [2019] | Series: New library of
psychoanalysis | Includes bibliographical references and index.
Identifiers: LCCN 2018059785 (print) | LCCN 2019001884 (ebook) |
ISBN 9780429261916 (Master) | ISBN 9780429524028 (Adobe) |
ISBN 9780429552199 (Mobipocket) | ISBN 9780429537493 (ePub3) |
ISBN 9780367205072 (hbk : alk. paper) | ISBN 9780367205089
(pbk : alk. paper) | ISBN 9780429261916 (ebk)
Subjects: LCSH: Psychoanalysts–Psychology.
Classification: LCC BF109.A1 (ebook) | LCC BF109.A1 S43 2019
(print) | DDC 150.19/5092–dc23
LC record available at https://lccn.loc.gov/2018059785

ISBN: 978-0-367-20507-2 (hbk)
ISBN: 978-0-367-20508-9 (pbk)
ISBN: 978-0-429-26191-6 (ebk)

Typeset in Bembo
by Swales & Willis, Exeter, Devon, UK

In loving memory of Jurek, Marysia, Paweł
and Michał

Contents

Acknowledgements

I have been extremely fortunate throughout my career to have had the help and support of exceptional teachers and mentors. I trained as a psychoanalytic psychotherapist at the Tavistock Clinic and was taught and supervised by outstanding clinicians such as David Malan, Peter Hildebrand and John Boreham. John Steiner's Borderline Workshop was particularly inspiring, and his personality and approach to clinical work stimulated in me an ambition to train as a psychoanalyst. At the British Psychoanalytic Society my supervisors were Adam Limentani and Anne-Marie Sandler and, later, Hanna Segal and Harold Stewart; my analyst was Martin Miller; their influence on my professional and personal development is inestimable. Since qualifying I have discussed my clinical work with Irma Brenman Pick, and my debt to her is great. Graham Ingham, my closest colleague, has been incredibly important as a colleague in the North of England and also as a friend. Beyond individuals, being a member of the British Society has provided me with a professional home, wonderful and creative colleagues and enormous support in developing psychoanalysis and psychoanalytic training in the North of England. I am also grateful to be an Honorary Member of the Polish Psychoanalytical Society and proud to have played a part in its development since the eighties.

I began writing this book when I was a Visiting Professor at Kyoto University in Japan and am grateful to that institution and to Professor Kunihiro Matsuki for his unfailing support. To Alessandra Lemma and some anonymous reviewers I owe gratitude for careful reading and trenchant and necessary criticism.

My greatest fortune has however been in my personal life. My family's educational and professional lives had been wrecked by the war, but they made sure that I could grow up with the opportunities they had been deprived of – I owe them such a lot. Jackie, Dan, Laura and George ensure that I have had, and continue to have, the happy settled and fulfilled home life that allows for the time, mental space and relative peace of mind that a psychoanalyst needs. A very sincere thank you to them.

I would also like to thank the *International Journal of Psychoanalysis* and Taylor & Francis, LLC, for their kind permission to reproduce the following copyright material:

"The dream space and countertransference". Vol. 78 (1997).
"The patient's material as an aid to the disciplined working through of the countertransference and supervision". Vol. 84 (2003).
"Discussion". Vol. 90 (2009).
"The psychoanalyst's normal and pathological superegos". Vol. 97 (2016).

INTRODUCTION

One reason I was attracted to psychoanalysis when I was a clinical psychologist was that its means of understanding can be applied to the clinician as readily as to the patient. Indeed the emphasis on gaining insight by attempting to become aware of the counter-transference means that psychoanalysts have a professional duty to attempt to understand themselves from a psychoanalytical vantage point. During training and then for many years after qualifying, I have been interested in the emotional demands that the practice of psychoanalysis makes upon the clinician. I have been able to study this in myself and I have also been engaged in the supervision of many practitioners, psychotherapists and psychoanalysts, both in training and after qualification. In particular my interest has focused on those factors which impede the clinician's ability to understand the patient, to intervene effectively and hence to promote emotional growth in the patient and, indirectly, in the analyst.

The day after the England football team had been knocked out of a World Cup tournament a patient came for her session and as she prepared to lie on the couch she noticed that I had a slight limp as I walked to my chair. As she lay down she said "Oh, limping are we?" in a *faux* sympathetic manner. My immediate reaction was the glancing thought: "What a bitch!" My patient had reason to believe I was interested in football since she had recently read that I was involved in a conference on Psychoanalysis and Sport and so she might have supposed that I was feeling sore about the English defeat. The session continued but it was only after the patient had left and I was writing up my notes that I recalled her comment and my impromptu unspoken response to her sarcasm at the beginning of the session. I then realised that I had done my patient a disservice since she had gone on to talk about how anxious she was about a

1

presentation she had to make later that day. She was worried that the audience would see the weaknesses in her argument and would not hesitate to criticise her. Had I been able to bear in mind her cruel treatment of me when seeing my weakness, I would have been able to take up in a more meaningful way her anxiety that others would put the boot into her if they were to see her having difficulties. The reason I had not been able to help her in this way was because I had repressed my awareness of her treatment of me, most probably because it made me feel hateful towards her.

My clinical vignette clearly places countertransference as central to an understanding of the patient. It also illustrates the nature of the countertransference experience: I described myself having a "glancing" thought, that is, a thought that did not sufficiently impose itself upon my mind and demand I attend to it. Very frequently the clinician's emotional response to the clinical situation does not even impinge itself to that degree; it remains unconscious for a significant period of time. My aim in this book is to explore some of the emotional difficulties and resistances that the psychoanalyst will have to encounter in himself in the course of his clinical work. I regard them as inevitable and believe that the clinician will have to struggle with these factors in his own personality as they arise in his contact with patients.

In exploring the nature of countertransference, many authors have written of the patient projecting a part of himself into the analyst; personally I don't this is a helpful way of describing the process. Rather than thinking of a patient projecting his experience or a part of his personality into the analyst I find it more helpful to think of a process in which the patient will evoke a potential aspect of the analyst's personality. Thus, it might be thought that my patient succeeded in bringing into play my potential to kick out when I am wounded in an (unsuccessful) attempt to help me understand her anxiety about her presentation later in the day. I don't think it very helpful to distinguish between the patient engaging a neurotic part of the analyst's personality and a different process whereby the countertransference can be used in order to understand the patient. Whether my instinctual reaction of wanting to kick back at my patient was pathological or not is not the issue; whether or not I could sufficiently register it in order to understand more deeply what then happened in the session is the more pertinent question.

Freud (1913, p. 320) wrote that "everyone possesses in his own unconscious an instrument with which he can interpret the utterances of the unconscious in other people". This will apply in the psycho-analytic setting and is the basis for the analyst's countertransference: "the patient's influence on [the analyst's] unconscious feelings" (Freud, 1910b, pp. 144–145). He added "no psychoanalyst goes further than his own complexes and his internal resistances allow". These statements, taken together, imply that the analyst will uncon-sciously understand what the patient's material means but the extent to which he will allow himself to become conscious of this will depend on "his internal resistances". While the countertransference will initially at least register unconsciously, it is uncertain whether the clinician will be able to allow it to reach conscious awareness; to the extent that he is not able to, the treatment will not be able to "go further", or, at least, not as a psychoanalytic treatment.

Of course, the analyst will also be aware that the patient too has "an instrument with which he can interpret the utterances of the unconscious in other people". In some circumstances this might be an additional reason why the analyst tries to limit his awareness of what is happening in the consulting room – he will attempt to hide, not only from himself but also from his patient, states of mind about which he might feel ashamed or guilty. I will give examples of these phenomena.

If negotiated productively, this working through of one's personality during the course of one's professional life can increase the competence of the psychoanalyst as he matures in his career. I intend to describe various such processes, but my arguments will focus on the central role of the analyst's superego as a structure that might impede either his understanding of the patient or, alternatively, support him as he struggles to understand the clinical material. I will also discuss the importance of a related internal structure, the ego ideal. I will offer a hypothetical model of how an emotional development may proceed in the course of a psychoanalytical career.

Another important theme in my vignette is that of aggression. Frequently a distinction is made between healthy aggression which can manifest itself in traits like ambition, competitiveness and drive (in the commonplace meaning of the word) on the one hand, and a more hostile and destructive sort which shows itself as envy, spoiling and self-harming acts. While the emphasis in the book is on the latter, it is also argued that a person becoming conscious of his more destructive aggression and its consequences can enable the development of a greater sense of reality and a greater capacity for love. Therefore it is an essential aspect of a psychoanalytic treatment and, it will be argued, one that can pose the greatest difficulties for the practitioner.

As Laplanche and Pontalis (1973) clarify, for at least the decade preceding *Beyond the Pleasure Principle* (1920), Freud was pre-occupied with the issues of hate, masochism and sadism. In "Instincts and their vicissitudes" (1915a, p. 138) he wrote that "the true prototypes of the relation of hate are derived not from sexual life, but from the ego's struggle to preserve and maintain itself"; he saw hate as a way of relating to objects and the self as "older than love" (p. 139). I take this to mean that in earliest infancy when the baby is confronted with a frustration that it can only experience as life threatening, then it responds with what we can call hate. It hates the registering of its experience and it hates whatever it is that is causing it. Thus the hatred is directed against the experiencing self and the external world, however that latter is portrayed in the infant's experience. Hate is a fundamental aspect of human experience.

A discussion among analysts about hatred, hostility and destructiveness can turn too quickly and too often to the usefulness, or not, of Freud's concept of the death instinct. Freud was persuaded to conceive the concept of a death instinct predominantly by clinical observation:

> If we take into consideration the whole picture made up of the phenomena of masochism immanent in so many people, the negative therapeutic reaction and the sense of guilt found in so many neurotics, we shall no longer be able to adhere to the belief that mental events are exclusively governed by the desire for pleasure. These phenomena are unmistakable indications of the presence of a power in mental life which we call the instinct of aggression or of destruction according to its aims, and which we trace back to the original death instinct of living matter.
>
> (1937, p. 243)

Laplanche and Pontalis suggested that Freud, beyond clinical observation, also felt "a speculative need which he consider[ed] to be fundamental ... we may suppose that ... Freud found hate particularly hard to integrate into the framework of an instinctual monism" (1973, pp. 97–103). Freud's recognition of hate and hostility as a fact of the human psyche was, to some extent, waylaid, I would suggest, by his need to offer a dualistic polarity between Eros and Thanatos. This theoretical issue has divided analytic communities, including the one in which I was trained. They became split between those who thought that the death instinct captured something very valuable about the human condition and those who judged it to be fantastical and not worthy of serious consideration.

It is my impression that some of those analysts who rejected the validity of the concept also, in some cases and to some degree, lost a focus on the issues of hatred and destructiveness. This may have been for reasons of a personal discomfort in confronting their patients' hostility, and their own, as much as for theoretical reasons. But as I will try to demonstrate with clinical examples throughout the book, an underlying acceptance of the general validity of the death instinct as a description of a basic hostility is not a sufficient condition to guarantee that destructiveness and hostility will always be perceived clearly by the clinician. I will argue that an anxiety about his own hostility may inhibit a clinician, as in my vignette, no matter what his theoretical position is on the issue of the death instinct. It is not only a theoretical disagreement which has left many analysts diminishing the role of aggression or destruction in clinical pathology but also a reluctance to perceive it and to take it into consideration. The patient's destructiveness or hostility poses specific difficulties in the countertransference, and it is an exploration of this that is one main aim of this book.

Chapter 1 is essentially a description of three clinical vignettes, the first from a consultation and the other two from extended analytic treatments. The aim of the chapter is primarily to describe what kind of change in a person's functioning a psychoanalytic treatment seeks to achieve. A second purpose is to indicate the kinds of emotional pressure the psychoanalyst will have to bear and work through in order to be able to intervene effectively. Two of the cases described were reported in a previous publication (Sedlak, 1997) in order to illustrate how the patients' and the analyst's dreams could be used in order to understand the patient and to work through difficulties in the countertransference. In the intervening years, as I developed as a psychoanalyst, I came to realise the material was open to a different and deeper interpretation. This concerns the patients' struggle with their hostility towards their objects, including the analyst, their guilt about this, and the corresponding countertransferential difficulty of engaging with these dynamics in a clinically effective way. The re-examination of this clinical material reveals the central importance of the superego on the patient's and the analyst's ability to register consciously their experience of each other in a way that is then conducive to understanding, interpretation and emotional growth.

Chapter 2 develops the theme of the analyst having to confront a resistance in himself in order to understand the patient with a focus on the analyst's superego. I draw a distinction between a pathological superego and a more benign structure, the normal superego which is concerned with moral judgement but takes into account ordinary human failings and can offer support to the struggling clinician. I trace the development of these concepts in Freud and Klein and some later authors. In this chapter I briefly review the concept of the death instinct and propose that it is useful as a means of describing a primitive hatred of frustration and psychic pain and of the parts of the self that register such experience. This allows me to draw attention to aggression and particularly its destructive and hostile manifestations and to suggest that the analyst himself, however well analysed, will continue to have the propensity to regress to this primitive state. I suggest that Strachey in his famous paper hesitated to clarify that the analyst will find it difficult to interpret effectively because he fears he will disclose his hostility to the patient. I argue for the usefulness and necessity of conceptualising a healthy, mature and reality-oriented superego. I demonstrate the difference between this mode of judging oneself and others on moral matters with the harshness and condemnation that come when the mature superego is superseded by an infantile or primitive superego. I contend that in the emotional cauldron that the analytic relationship can be, the analyst has to beware of his capacity to regress to this primitive form of judgement and act this out in the form of an interpretation, given not in order to help the patient understand himself better but in order to criticise and punish him.

Chapter 3 develops this argument further, and I contend that the analyst, in his dread of becoming punitive may mute his clinical acumen and may need some time and even outside help from a colleague in order to be able to realise what is going on and treat it with some equanimity. I also review briefly some analytic literature which suggests that the wish or need to pass judgement on oneself and others is ubiquitous and has to be considered by the psychoanalyst in his daily work. I review Freud's concept of dread as clarified in the "Uncanny" paper (1919) and suggest that the superego is clearly implicated in Freud's understanding of dread. These ideas are illustrated by a description of a clinical case.

When I presented an earlier version of Chapter 2 to a Scientific Meeting of the British Society, Edna O'Shaughnessy acknowledged the importance of the superego and pointed out that there was a related concept that might throw further light on the issues I was investigating. She meant the ego ideal, a relatively neglected psychoanalytical concept. In Chapter 4 I review the origins of the concept and suggest reasons why it has largely fallen out of usage. I then describe what the analyst's ego ideals may be and how they may conflict with each other under the pressures imposed by the clinical situation. I also consider how the analyst's struggles with this conflict may be observed by the patient and play their part in clinical progress. Clinical vignettes are given to illustrate the arguments.

Due to the fact that psychoanalysis is a relatively young discipline and its field of study, the human mind, is so complex, failures of psychoanalytical endeavour are not rare, and in Chapter 5 I report on two analytic treatments that I would consider as failed analyses. I attempt to understand what factors in the patient and the analyst ensured that the treatments broke down and contend that in both cases the patient felt that an assessment of the reality of their situation would expose them to a sense of a catastrophic failure in measuring up to their ego ideals and hence a damning and dangerous confrontation with a pathological superego; in short, I came to believe that both patients feared they might become suicidal if they continued their treatment. In these cases I felt as sure as I could be that I was able to remain empathic to their dilemma but, since the countertransference is largely an unconscious phenomenon, I was unable to tell whether something in my attitude led either patient to feel that their underlying hostility to themselves was shared by their analyst. I include this material in the book since I believe that the consideration of therapeutic failure is an essential aspect of a clinician's development and can serve not only as a base for new learning but also as part of a necessary and realistic container of therapeutic ambition. It is an experience of loss of the wished-for objects, including an analyst who remains equitable at all times, a patient who improves and a clinical practice which is always effective. It is an experience of narcissistic loss and an injury to the ego ideal and the view of oneself as clinically effective. It is an experience of disappointment in psychoanalysis or at least in the psychoanalysis the practitioner himself can offer. I suggest that these experiences are inevitable and, if worked through well, can help the analyst have realistic aspirations in his work and hence be less liable to be hostile when confronted with seemingly insurmountable clinical difficulties.

My focus on the difficulties the therapist will experience in allowing himself to become conscious of the emotional situation between himself and his patient has implications for the practice of supervision, and this is the subject of Chapter 6. I review how the psychoanalytic training institutes differed in their views about the propriety of the personal analyst also being the supervisor, of at least the third training case, in what were called control analyses. While the view that this should not become standard practice prevailed, a related view, that the supervisor should have a stated therapeutic intention, to the extent of enquiring into the supervisee's personal history, has present day adherents. They argue that this allows for a deeper understanding of the countertransference and the difficulties it poses for the therapist. I maintain that this this view is erroneous and give two examples of supervision, one of them being the supervision of a practitioner with no experience of his own personal therapy, to illustrate the point that even in such circumstances the supervisor can be effective without straying into the role of the supervisee's therapist. Indeed, I try to illustrate that paradoxically the supervisee's trust that the supervisor will not attempt an approach that would be akin to analysing the supervisee allows the latter to be more open about the countertransference. This is not the same as arguing that good supervision cannot be therapeutic but rather that the personal insight and working through that the supervision may instigate, has to be properly left to the supervisee to do, or not, beyond the purview of the supervisor.

Comparing different theoretical and technical psychoanalytical approaches is fraught with difficulties since each approach is embedded in its own historical, geographical and cultural context, and unless one is aware of this then it is easy to misunderstand an approach other than one's own. Furthermore the fact that every clinician will have his limitations will mean that his efforts to help the patient will be circumscribed; inevitably then every clinician has to struggle with a conscious or unconscious sense of failure and guilt. If this is unbearable then it may be projected and manifest itself as a criticism of other approaches – one reason, I argue, that disputes amongst analysts can become so heated. I acknowledge these difficulties at the beginning of Chapter 7. Nevertheless, I suggest that reports of clinical work, particularly if they include a convincing indication of the analyst's countertransference during the session(s), can allow for tentative comparisons between different approaches to be made. Such comparisons are necessary for the development of psychoanalysis as a clinical method which has at least some evidential or experiential basis. I look at two different theoretical and technical approaches from the point of view that is central to this book, namely that a clinician has to struggle to manage the countertransference and in particular when the patient's presentation provokes the crueller version of the analyst's superego. I first consider a historical example of the difficulties that can arise in such a situation and suggest that Freud was unable to manage his countertransference in a way that could have been clinically useful in his treatment of the Wolf Man. I then re-visit a debate I was able to have with Jessica Benjamin when she presented a paper on her approach to the British Psychoanalytical Society; this became one of the series of "Psychoanalytical Controversies" published in the *International Journal of Psychoanalysis*. Benjamin's approach is a development of Kohut's self psychology, and I examine critically some of Kohut's claims about his theoretical and technical innovations, arguing that they developed precisely because of a difficulty in managing a critical attitude to a patient's narcissistic and hostile presentation.

In the last thirty years or so a number of approaches, developed separately, have introduced a technical innovation which stresses the analyst's ability to find a representation in his mind for mental states which, it is argued, the patient cannot represent and hence begin to be able to bear. I look at one such specific approach, developed in France by César and Sára Botella, and examine their reported clinical material. I contend that it demonstrates the analyst's difficulty in giving thought to the patient's murderous hostility and that their approach can be understood as the analyst having to contain a pathological superego and transform it into a normal superego.

Chapter 8 is entitled "Hostility terminable and interminable". I review psychoanalytic literature which supports the view that the working through of one's hostility is necessary and a developmental achievement which promotes a capacity for love and a diminution of narcissistic relating to the world and hence a greater contact with reality. I then present two cases in some depth. The first of these demonstrates what on the whole can be viewed as a successful analysis in which the clinical work enabled a convincing development of the patient's personality. The second, on the contrary, was ended prematurely by the patient, and I suggest that one reason for this was my inability to grasp fully the depth of the patient's hostility and the catastrophe she feared if she were to give it up.

Ever since I read Bion's (1970, p. 9) distinction between suffering from a mental state and being able to suffer it, I have thought that, in that simple statement, he beautifully conveyed a central aim of psychoanalysis. For the psychoanalyst it means developing a personality which has the resilience to suffer what the patient inflicts upon the analyst; my example at the beginning of this introduction is an example of not being able to suffer the patient's attack. I would contend that until the analyst can suffer the patient, the treatment he can offer can only be superficial or intellectual. If he can suffer however, then he can begin to speak to the patient in a way that can help the patient suffer his emotional states rather than suffer from them. The development usually has to begin in the analyst, and it is a consideration of the difficulties this imposes upon the clinician that is a central theme of this book.

As I delved into the psychoanalytic literature in researching this book I was constantly struck by its richness and the depth of thought that many analysts have applied, not only to their treatment of patients, but also to their struggles with themselves in doing the work. The accumulation of papers and books on the central problem of containing and understanding the countertransference is a testament to that. I do not claim therefore that the reasoning and argumentation in this book are original; rather, it is more that I highlight a problem that I have observed in myself and in other analysts and therapists with whom I have discussed clinical work. I have tried not to fall into the trap of claiming a *pars pro toto* for my thesis but I do think that it elucidates a problem in professional and personal development that many clinicians will recognise.

Providing clinical examples which illustrate theoretical arguments is a necessary part of promoting the serious consideration of the ideas being put forward. Immediately one runs into a seemingly unresolvable dilemma. One has promised the patient, explicitly or implicitly, confidentiality; seemingly then to report aspects of their personalities, histories and difficulties, even with a scientific purpose, will almost always be felt as a breach of trust. Kantrowitz (2004) has researched and discussed the dilemmas and complications of publishing clinical material with great sensitivity. The International Psychoanalytical Association (2018) has also produced a very carefully researched document on these issues. Gaining consent from the patient is not without its problems, since the request is made within a situation in which transference and countertransference (both largely unconscious) predominate; it is not possible to know what the granting of permission really means in these circumstances, what pressures asking for it imposes on the patient, and with what long term consequences. I have chosen not to ask my patients for permission to give my version of what occurred between us. I have disguised their identities to the point that I believe they would not be identifiable to their closest acquaintances or family members and, I hope, even to themselves. If they do happen to recognise themselves (for example in the reporting of specific details of a dream) then I hope they feel that I have tried to convey the material as truthfully as I could and with a purpose of promoting scientific debate and progress. I believe the ideas I have put forward in this book will be helpful to some clinicians and their dissemination will, in a small way, facilitate the development of psychoanalytical technique. Of course, the narcissistic motivation involved in publishing one's ideas cannot be denied, and for this I can only ask for my patients' understanding and forbearance.

Throughout the book I have used the pronoun "he" and the possessive pronoun "his" to denote both genders except when it is clear that I am referring to a female. While I wished to avoid sexist language, writing "he/she" and "his/her" proved too clumsy, as did the use of "they" and "their" as a means of avoiding gendered pronouns.

1

THE AIMS OF PSYCHOANALYTIC TREATMENT

Introduction

The means by which a psychoanalytic treatment aspires to relieve suffering have been variously conceptualised. Money-Kyrle (1968, 1971) described three different aims of psychoanalytic treatment and the chronological order in which they developed. Freud's initial understanding of neurosis centred on the inhibition of sexual desire and his therapeutic intent was to undo this inhibition. Modifying his theory in the light of clinical experience Freud then developed his second model of therapeutic intent which was based on an understanding of the forces which led to repression in the patient. This model, which is essentially one of moral conflict, is still one of the major tenets underlying psychoanalytical understanding of mental suffering. This conceptualisation was further strengthened by Freud's introduction of the tripartite structure of the mind which emphasised the conflict between forces from the id (whether sexual or destructive) and the strictures on thought and behaviour imposed by the force of the superego. Fajrajzen (2014) noted that all of Freud's reported clinical cases could be conceptualised as suffering from moral dilemmas.

Money-Kyrle (1968) argued that a third model had emerged, also based on conflict, but this time on the conflict between the patient's wishes and the strictures of reality. This was implicit in Freud's conceptualisation of disavowal (Freud, 1927), which Freud had described as a means of dealing with the anxiety raised by the perception of the female lack of a penis, but Money-Kyrle (1971) focused on three other fundamental aspects of reality. He argued that there were other essential realities which are resisted or whose truth is perverted in one way or another: the fact that the breast is a supremely good thing upon which one's life is utterly dependent; the reality that one only came into being because one was created within the Oedipal situation; and thirdly, that death is inevitable. It could be argued that all three realities also contain the essence of narcissistic pain since all three speak of the limitations of one's omnipotence and in all three there is the implicit acknowledgement of the separate existence of the object(s).

Bion reportedly said that the aim of psychoanalytic treatment was to introduce the patient to the person who they were destined to spend the rest of their life with, namely to their own self. While this certainly indicated the epistemological aim of psychoanalytic treatment, essentially of getting to know oneself, it should be clear that such knowledge will also have an emotional counterpart. If an analysis is to help the patient function better in life then it must also enable knowledge about oneself to be bearable. For instance, awareness that one is envious and destructive of others' abilities must be contained by a mind that can suffer guilt without becoming self-hating and self-destructive. Equally, awareness of one's ability to be successful should not lead to an attack on one's achievements due to the guilt of doing better than others; some patients need help in being able to "suffer" their good fortune.

I am going to present three clinical cases which illustrate how coming to know oneself better involves the overcoming of a resistance which frequently has a moral basis. I intend to show that in the course of the work the psychoanalyst too has to overcome resistances to knowing himself and in particular knowing and tolerating his experience of the patient. In the first case this proved to be reasonably uncomplicated, in part because the patient was relatively healthy psychologically but also because the analyst had sufficiently worked through the issues raised so as to be able to contain them and subject them to thought. The following two cases demonstrate the more usual state of affairs in which the analyst has to struggle over time to orient himself to his experience with the patient.

Clinical example: Mr A

By way of introduction to how the themes outlined above will be developed in this book I will describe a consultation I conducted with a man in his early thirties.

13

A young university lecturer was referred to me because he was depressed and his general practitioner thought that he could benefit from understanding himself better, rather than from a pharmacological approach. When I met him he told me that he had first suffered from depression when he was twenty-four, at a time when he and his girl-friend had lived abroad as part of his doctoral studies. They were in a beautiful country, they were in love and yet he became very depressed, to the point that his dejection and withdrawal from her ruined their relationship and she left him and returned to England. Now, four years later, he had just secured a lecturing post, and this was a considerable achievement, but he felt threatened by depression again. At one point I said to him that there seemed to be a pattern – he became depressed when things were going well for him. In response, he told me that when he was twelve his father had been diagnosed with a neurological illness that meant he had deteriorated physically until he was now unable to walk or speak and needed constant care. The patient said that this had spurred him on to do well, and his successes in life (he was a skilled sportsman as well as being academically successful) had been the one thing that his mother and father could take pleasure in. His mother in particular often told him that his achievements enabled her to keep going in the face of the tragedy that had befallen their family.

He began the second consultation session by complaining that I did not ask him questions, he did not know what to say, he wondered whether I was the right person to help him; perhaps he would do better by pulling himself together and getting on with it. The first part of the session was very difficult, and I could see he was very dissatisfied and also anxious and at one stage I thought he might walk out of the session. However, and somewhat reluctantly, he then told me a dream. *He was at a meeting with his senior professor who was dressed formally but whose shoes were covered in mud. A young female colleague also noticed this and they exchanged glances, it was important that they did not let the professor see that they had noticed his dirty feet.* He had two thoughts related to the dream, the first was that he had first noticed that his father was ill when he was twelve and they had been playing football together. He noticed his father's feet were not as well co-ordinated as they had been; this had been one of the first symptoms of his illness. The second association to the dream was that he had seen the professor looking at the young female colleague in an admiring way; he thought the professor was attracted to her.

14

At this point the patient became anxious and said that of course it was perfectly possible for an older man to be in a relationship with a younger woman. As he said this he looked nervously at me, and it seemed clear to me he was anxious and was reassuring me in case I had been personally offended by what he had said about older men. I guessed the professor and I were about the same age, also probably the age of his father. He then said that he was anxious today because he had to give his first lecture in the afternoon; he dreaded making a mess of it.

As I listened to him recounting his dream, I had had an association: it was to the saying "to have feet of clay"; that is to present oneself as strong while actually not having much substance and in fact being weak. So I said to him that we were now in a situation in which he was anxious that I would see that he thought I might not be powerful enough to help him and he was worried that I would notice that he might take this view of me, just as he was worried in the dream that the professor would see that he had noticed his dirty feet. He agreed with that and said that his doctor said I had a good reputation, but he feared that I would prove to be not much good, at least in being able to help him. I went on to say that he was very frightened to think that he could reveal that I was weak and that he was stronger and more able than me: for instance that he might be able to pull himself together without my help, or, another example, that in reality his young colleague would be attracted to him and not to me or his professor.

He looked interested in this and said "yes". He looked thoughtful for a few moments and then told me that when he suffered his first depression he and his then girlfriend had gone on a walk in the mountains – they had climbed very high onto a ridge and looked down over a fantastic landscape and he had felt so lucky to be there with her. He had then suddenly become extremely anxious and was terrified of the height and that he might fall. He had never before suffered from vertigo and his girlfriend had to hold him tight, reassure him that he was safe and help him down. It was after this incident that his depression, which eventually ruined their relationship, began.

I said to him that he became very frightened when he did get high and I thought this gave us an insight into his difficulty with me and in his life at the moment. I interpreted that when he did get high he thought he could look down on me as someone who might not be able to help him as well as he could help himself. In the same way he might look down onto his professor who is revealed to be interested in a much younger woman. I suggested that this might also be the way that he, as a twelve year old boy would have wished to look down on his father. After all, what healthy twelve year old boy would not wish to show himself to be a better footballer than his father? The patient now became intensely thoughtful and said "I feel so ... so ... guilty". He then said again "I feel so ... so ... I don't know what to call it". I said to him that he had said exactly how he felt: so guilty.

As at that time I had no vacancies I referred Mr A to another analyst with whom he went on have a successful analysis. My colleague informed me that the dynamics that were briefly explored in the two consultation sessions with me were central in the analysis.

Discussion of Mr A

I want to use this material to highlight certain themes which will be developed further in this book. The vignette can be used to draw the distinction between suffering from something and being able to suffer something. The patient was unable to suffer guilt, he could not let himself know how guilty he felt as this was too painful for him; even when he correctly acknowledged his guilt he retracted the word and said "I don't know what to call it". He felt guilty because he did have aggressive competitive wishes towards his father, he also had them towards me: he started the second session by suggesting that he might be able to better cure himself without my help. This also became clearer when he described the dream and became worried that he had revealed that the Oedipal situation between us was one in which he was the young man who could get the girl while I was the older man who would lose in such a competition.

If he had been luckier his father would have remained healthy and their relationship would have been strong enough to accommodate the son's wish to be a man and to be bigger and better. Unfortunately he had fallen disastrously ill. The boy's guilt about his aggressive wishes were not worked through and became unconscious and therefore all the more powerful. Without knowing it, he then suffered from guilt – each time things went well for him he unconsciously punished himself: in the first instance he lost his girlfriend; when he came to see me he was anxious that he

16

might make a mess of the new job he had just achieved. This anxiety was evident in the session: he was worried he would make a mess of his lecture and I think he might indeed have done so if he had left the session with a feeling that he had succeeded in his attempt to dismiss me as being unable to help.

In this instance I was able to see what he was doing and I did not collapse. Instead I tried to show him that he felt guilty and show him why he felt like that. This put him in touch with his feeling of guilt and for a few moments he was able to feel guilt: "I feel so ... so ... guilty". This is what could be called suffering guilt instead of suffering from unconscious guilt.

One reason he was able to do this was because he felt that I could suffer the experience of being attacked by him or being triumphed over by him. I was able to realise that he wanted to put me down and to know this without reacting to it vengefully. When I spoke to him it was not with the purpose of showing him that I was the more able man; that intent would have played some part in my motivation since I am usually competitive, but my main purpose was to inform him about himself. I did not criticise him for doing this to me and nor did I say that it did not matter and so don't worry about it. I thought he *did* have to worry about it because it was the thing he unconsciously worried about anyway: that he triumphed over and diminished other older men or father figures.

I had to bear or suffer my feelings about being older and less attractive than my patient. This was in order to be reasonably sure that when I interpreted to him, my intention was to say something to him which communicated an understanding about him. I needed to safeguard against the possibility that my interpretation could be an attempt on my part to show him that I was, after all and despite his attempts, a stronger and more able man than he was. In so doing I had to be reasonably aware of truths about myself. I had to balance awareness of my own competitiveness against my wish to communicate an understanding to him. This is not to say that my motives would have been 100 per cent pure but that on balance the wish to communicate was stronger than the wish to demonstrate dominance. So my interpretation was not totally neutral of my wish to show who was the alpha male but it tended sufficiently in that direction.

This vignette is an illustration of what Money-Kyrle (1956) called the "normal" use of the countertransference. He wrote: "As the patient speaks, the analyst will, as it were, become introjectively identified with him, and having understood him inside, will re-project and interpret" (p. 361). My awareness of my own competitiveness allowed me pre-consciously to put myself in my patient's shoes and to identify briefly with him in order to understand him. I did not then have to do much working through in the countertransference, and this is frequently the case: the analyst should have worked through a good deal of his pathology so it is not too troublesome. Thus I sensed that he was provoking some kind of inter-generational battle but I had sufficiently worked through my feelings about ageing (through suffering) not to need too much to put the young man in his place. In the session I could suffer, that means bear or tolerate, the experience of being attacked by him or being triumphed over by him.

It is noteworthy how longer clinical contact with patients will usually expose the analyst to dilemmas which are not yet worked through, or that have to be re-engaged with as if they had not been encountered before. The vignette I have given occurred in a two session consultation; deeper difficulties are likely to emerge in ongoing analyses as I shall demonstrate below. (Alternatively the analyst may be in a somewhat different state of mind when seeing a patient for a consultation, perhaps more active, more investigatory and hence less vulnerable to the patient's projections.)

I remember when I was training saying to Edna O'Shaughnessy, one of my seminar leaders, that she had very quickly grasped the central issue of a session I had presented. I had wondered how my patient would have fared if he had been in analysis with her. She said that she thought it very likely that he would not have made any greater progress under her care since patients tend to discern unconsciously the extent of their analyst's understanding and then: "they pitch their material beyond that point"! She then made it clear that she thought that they did not do this necessarily out of a sense of spite or an unconscious wish to thwart the analyst but frequently because they sensed that they needed their analyst to struggle with dilemmas that they themselves could not work through. I now turn to such a case.

Clinical example: Mr B

Mr B came for analysis in his mid-forties. As a teenager and in his twenties he had enjoyed great success as an entrepreneur and he had in effect retired at the age of twenty-eight. However it was also at this time that his father had died, and hence this "retirement" was open to the interpretation that he had suffered a breakdown. This was relevant to his presentation at the beginning of the analysis in that his mother was then in her seventies and had been diagnosed as having an inoperable carcinoma. He told me in the consultation interviews that he feared he would not be able to cope with her death. He had also just suffered the breakdown of a relationship with a much younger, very glamorous woman who had left him for a younger man, a blow that had hit him very hard and which had also reinforced his anxieties about his ageing. He claimed that it had also left him physically disfigured by two marks on his face. He complained in his consultation that his mother was unsympathetic to the pain this caused him and mocked him for wearing make-up in his attempts to hide these marks.

I do not intend to give a full account of the analysis up to the point at which the series of incidents I want to describe occurred. In the first three years of the analysis a convincing picture emerged of a man who was persecuted by an underlying phantasy that his resources could at any point be lost to him. In his childhood he had developed the habit of holding on to his stools and in adulthood he still took an exceptional interest in his toileting. He worried obsessively about money although he continued to be very comfortably off; he was extremely careful about expending his physical, mental and emotional energies. He had very many complicated routines and rituals that were designed to save time but which inevitably made him late for most appointments including his sessions. He was persecuted by the sense that time was slipping away from him. Although he himself acknowledged that he had in effect spent sixteen years doing almost nothing, he told me that in that time he was forever racing against the clock.

As might be imagined, Mr B hated paying for his analysis, particularly for those rare sessions that he was unable to attend. Nevertheless he did appear to make some progress in his life during the first three years of the treatment. His skin complaint had quickly cleared up, and he developed a new relationship with a woman only a little younger than himself. This was difficult and characterised by much to-ing and fro-ing but, as far as I could tell, also had many good qualities. He also began to work again, for the first time in about twenty years, on a much smaller scale than before but in a way that gave him much satisfaction, particularly when he could report that his earnings from this work more than covered the cost of his analysis.

During the first three years of the analysis his mother's health had slowly deteriorated. His attempts to take her to faith healers and to persuade her to try ever more far-fetched therapies had slowly subsided in the face of analytic work which helped him face the reality of her deterioration. He slowly came to accept the fact of her approaching death and began to devote his energies, together with those of his two sisters, to making her last days as comfortable and as pain-free as they could arrange. One Friday morning a message was left on my answering-machine by his partner to say that his mother was in the process of dying and he would not attend his session.

He rang me that same afternoon to say that she had died in the morning just at the time that his session began. We spoke for a few minutes and, in the course of our conversation, I said that the care that he and his sisters had given his mother in her last months (which had really impressed me very much) must have helped her enormously. He thanked me for this and for the help I had given him in facing his mother's death. The following Monday Mr B told me that he had spoken to his partner about our telephone conversation and of his appreciation of what I had said to him. She had responded by saying "Oh yes, but he'll still charge you for the missed session". Mr B added that he had told her he knew that of course I would not do such a thing. Upon hearing this I immediately felt ambushed; I had always charged Mr B for missed sessions, it had always been a contentious issue, and now I felt that he was taking advantage of these exceptional circumstances in order to make his long-held point that it was unreasonable of me to charge him for those sessions he could not attend.

I was also aware that he had spoken to me with a certain guile and that he knew he was putting me in a most difficult situation. Certainly it felt a heinous thing to do to charge a patient for missing a session to be with his literally dying mother. I resisted the powerful temptation to say "Of course I won't charge you" and decided to sit tight, most of all because I felt that I had been trapped into an almost impossible situation. I soon resolved that, heinous though it might be, I would charge him for that session, and then I had to face the music. He was appalled by my callousness, greed, insensitivity, and over the next few weeks he would regularly convince me that I was indeed as he imagined me to be. He spoke with many of his relations and friends (some of whom were solicitors, one a specialist in fraud cases, he told me) who were equally affronted by my behaviour. Despite my great discomfort at times, I was sure that something very important was happening, especially when the patient began to intersperse his complaints about me with reports of a recurring dream, or rather a recurring failure to have a dream. He had very rarely brought dreams to his analysis, and this was more in the nature of a nightmare. *He was standing next to his mother's grave; out of the ground came decomposing arms that grasped him and pulled him into the coffin and next to her decomposing body.* When the dream reached this point he would regularly wake in a sweat and with his heart beating very fast. I noticed that as Mr B told me this he would squirm on the couch as though he felt that what he was describing was actually happening to him and he would cover his eyes in his attempts to shield himself from these images. He began to fear that they would enter his mind at any point of the day or night, as indeed they increasingly did.

Tentatively I tried to link the arms that grasped and then pulled him into the grave with what he felt to be my grasping nature (in that part of Northern England "grasping", as well as its usual meaning, has a very particular meaning of taking greedily for financial benefit). Mr B usually understood such interpretations as my trying to deflect from the unarguable fact that the present situation had indeed revealed me to be grasping, and for a number of weeks the analysis floundered in this extremely uncomfortable atmosphere. At the end of the month he paid his bill, but I felt that the analysis might well have broken down at that point.

Over time I noticed that Mr B's manner to me became slightly warmer – mainly, I thought, because he was becoming increasingly worried about the intrusive images that his nightmares created. At the same time my analytic interest in what was going on became greater than my personal discomfort at the thought of having charged him for that session. As my countertransference altered in this way, one day with much difficulty, Mr B told me that at his mother's funeral, which had occurred on the Sunday following her death and hence before the session in which the storm about his fees broke, as the coffin had been lowered into the grave he had had the "terrible" thought: "I wonder what she left me in her will?" As he said this he shuddered much as he did whenever he described his images of his mother's decomposing body. I took up with him how awful he felt about himself for having such a thought, and he elaborated upon his feeling that everybody at the funeral would have been appalled at him were they to know about it. Interestingly he later came to link the thought he had had at the funeral with an intrusive image he had frequently experienced when giving his mother a drink in her last years: that of throwing the hot tea into her face. This was part of a development in which he became more conscious of his aggression, his greed and the way he had always defended himself against knowing about this, particularly in relation to his mother.

Mr B's nightmare images receded after the work described above and he was free of them from that time. It was not the case that he came to thank me for making my stand about his fee; he continued to resent paying for missed sessions and the annual raising of his fee was always a painful process. However, it was consequently more possible for him to consider various aspects of his character such as his greed and his wish to exert total control over his environment. Useful work was done in linking the above themes to the issue of his ageing and over the course of the next three years he became more flexible and less persecuted in his relationship to time. His relationship with his partner matured further, and he became far more tolerant of the normal physical imperfections of her middle-aged body, which had bothered him greatly at the beginning of their relationship.

This period of analysis illustrates how a patient who was so over-whelmed by a piece of psychic reality (about his own acquisitiveness and aggression) that he could not face it, had to project it into other objects. He attempted to do this into the object of his mother's body, but this was not successful; he could not dream this, and it became a nightmare that woke him and an image that haunted him. He projected it into his analyst, who then had to bear the very disturbing feelings that he was heinous, "grasping", concerned more for his pocket than his patient's welfare and that everyone who might come to know of this would abhor him. It was only after I had borne these feelings until they were detoxified and began to be a source of some professional interest that the patient was able to admit to himself the thought that he too could be "grasping". Such acknowledgement of his own nature in turn detoxified his external world. Significantly, this also eventually led to some change in his paranoia about the passage of time, so that he no longer felt so persecuted by the limits it placed upon him.

Discussion of Mr B

My experience with Mr B illustrates Money-Kyrle's (1956) point that the analyst first experiences the countertransference as primarily his own personal problem. Disentangling one's individual contribution to the countertransference from the patient's impact is frequently a complicated matter. For a number of weeks I was very uneasy about my conduct and then came to realise that I was anxious about the possibility that my commitment to maintaining the setting of the treatment, including the parameter of his paying for a missed session, was essentially a product of my personal need to feel professionally potent and correct. At the time, I had recently moved to a geographical location away from London and so I not only felt professionally isolated, but I was also concerned that my analytic standards would drop without collegial support. Mr B, I am sure, took advantage of this uncertainty to promote the feeling in me that I was acting unethically; his need to project his anxiety that he was more concerned for himself than for his object thus found a ready home in me. It was only after some working through in the countertransference that I was able to own this personal dilemma and balance its importance against the clinical significance of the unfolding events. I could then take some satisfaction from this and feel relief that I had, after all, been properly concerned with maintaining a professional and psychoanalytical standard for the benefit of my patient, as well as enacting a personal concern.

Clearly my ability to work through in the countertransference was significantly more difficult and prolonged than in Mr A's case, and in part this might indicate the relative level of disturbance in the two patients. However, I think it also illustrates a fact of psychoanalytic practice and the mutual enactment that occurs in the analytic situation. I once heard Ron Britton say that a clinician can see a patient for a consultation, even an extended one, and be able to speak with him and be heard by him with a certain degree of objectivity and interest. However when one engages in a longer term treatment the therapist inevitably "becomes It", as Britton put it, and is experienced, not as an objective outsider with an interesting and potentially helpful viewpoint, but as a transference figure.

In Mr B's case the transference figure he created had a very particular characteristic, namely a "grasping" nature, but sometimes the analytic situation reveals a much more comprehensive and all-encompassing transference situation, and this was the case with Mr C.

Clinical example: Mr C

Mr C was a professional man who was in his middle thirties when he came into treatment. He sought analysis because of a longstanding depression that he dated back to his childhood. From what I could gather, his parents had been disturbed in their own right. His mother appeared to take a paranoid view of the world and had suffered two major depressive breakdowns that had required hospitalisation. The first of these was at the time of a move of house which closely followed the birth of his sister. He was then four years old and he had vague memories from that time of feeling at a loss, in an unfamiliar place and with no one to help him. His father was described as a cold and controlling man. An older brother had been diagnosed as psychotic. His bleak emotionally cold childhood was best conveyed by his recollection of family meals, which were silent sombre affairs at which his father, if in a bad mood, might snap at any member of the family who was eating "wrongly".

The session I am going to present occurred six months after the beginning of his analysis. These months had been notable for the extreme care he took in speaking to me, his slow ponderous accounts of what he had done the previous day and his inability to feel at ease or to say anything to me spontaneously. In fact the few details about his life I have conveyed above I learnt at a later time, once he was able to talk a little more freely.

In this initial period he had only reported one dream in which he was standing in front of a mock Tudor house. His one association to this had been that he had always lived in Victorian houses, and I had interpreted how he felt that he was, in the analysis, always confronted with a victor who he felt was likely to mock him unless he was very careful about what he said. This interpretation had not relieved him but had seemed to increase the care he took in speaking to me. In the transference, despite my sympathy for his plight, I would find myself bored, impatient, and frequently my concentration would wander. This session came just after a weekend and in the week before a three-week Easter break which was the second holiday break he had experienced in the analysis.

24

I had noticed his difficulty in speaking getting progressively worse as the break approached, and in the previous Friday session he had begun to say that at work he had felt angry with a colleague but he had strangulated the word and said "ang ..." and had then stopped. I was reminded of this in this session by his tortuous way of speaking as he slowly described that over the weekend he had found himself very busy, doing too much, rushing around until he had a headache. I made a comment based on some material from the previous week about his anxiety about having too much time and feeling alone in an empty space. He responded to this by saying he was resigned to the Easter break, as one would be in a condemned cell. This remark led me to say that he felt Easter was the punishment for some crime he had committed. At this moment the patient spontaneously remembered a dream he had had the previous night. *He was walking along a railway line that ran along a raised embankment. Looking down he could see a robbery taking place; one man was stealing from another. Somehow he slipped down off the embankment, making his presence known to the robber who then pointed his gun at him and was about to shoot him.* He told me that at this point he had woken, feeling very anxious.

There was one association to the dream, which was that as an adolescent he had been a keen train–spotter. He and a friend had once walked across several tracks that had been electrified, they had had to take great care in stepping over them and his friend had nearly tripped onto a live rail. This association seemed to contain such an accurate description of the great care the patient took in speaking to me that I interpreted that he felt he had to be extremely careful in what he told me of his thoughts particularly in ensuring that he did not touch anything alive. I went on to suggest that the live emotion was the anger he felt about his belief that I was robbing him by taking a break but that he was terrified to show this because he felt it would lead to a deadly confrontation.

The patient did not respond to this for a number of minutes but he did shift around on the couch as if he was extremely uncomfortable. He then said "I feel hunted". The silence continued until in a most hesitant way he said that in the previous break he had felt nothing for a few days but had then felt extremely irritated. This last word was said only after a struggle in which he stuttered and finally forced the word out. This noticeably increased his physical discomfort. I interpreted that he felt that the dream had in effect happened in the session: he had been progressing carefully, keeping his feelings about my robbing him to himself and thus keeping himself above a dangerous confrontation. But then he had slipped, he had remembered his dream and had told me it and this had allowed me to see how he viewed the situation between us. He now felt that I had him in my sights and there was no escape. The patient's anxiety was not relieved by this interpretation, he repeated that he felt hunted and chaotic, and there the session finished. At the door the patient turned to me in his habitual way to say goodbye but this time said "OK, goodbye".

This material illustrates the patient's inability at this time to form a dream that would depict his dilemma and also serve the function of preserving his sleep. His capacity to do this had broken down in the night; hence his dream had changed into a nightmare that had woken him. In dynamically the same way he was unable to maintain a symbolic level of interchange with me in the session; again he suddenly found himself in the middle of a situation in which he felt concretely threatened, "hunted" as he put it. Although his saying "OK" before "goodbye" probably indicated that there still existed a part of his mind able to maintain the idea that what had occurred had been necessary and maybe even valuable, or at least OK, I think that for the most part he had felt concretely involved in a dangerous confrontation.

It was only after some further months that I was able to see for myself that my patient was actually putting me into the same position as he had occupied in the dream and that for a considerable period of time I was little better equipped to work through this dilemma than he was himself. Thus I slowly came to realise that a regular countertransferential experience was that I would feel robbed of what I felt was rightfully mine, i.e. the patient's free associations. This would often occur right at the beginning of a session when he would be silent but I sensed that he was thoughtful. However, after a few minutes he would begin to speak, but it would be to say, in a most flat way, "Yesterday ...", and he would then proceed to tell me what had happened the previous day. This would soon leave me feeling bored and inattentive. However, I would then be in a dilemma: if I tried to ignore this feeling and make myself concentrate I would find myself making interpretations that felt sterile and lifeless. This was hardly surprisingly, since I would have taken care to avoid the live rail/dynamic. If I did try to take up with him how he excluded me from his thinking we would quickly get into what

26

felt like a more deadly confrontation in which he felt very accused and caught out and would then proceed to berate himself in a vicious way.

As I was trying to think my way through this dilemma, in my supervision and at times by myself, I had a dream about the patient. I dreamt that *I was opening the door to him and, as I did so, he rushed past me and ran into the main part of the house. I was taken by surprise, felt shocked by the intrusion and quite unable to stop him.* It was clear in the dream that, having rushed past me, the patient continued past the consulting room door and the waiting room entrance, in fact the first two doors in the hallway, and hence past the boundary in the hall between the space set aside for patients and the family living space. As I thought about this dream I came to realise that it depicted very accurately my difficulties with this patient. His intrusive projection of his dilemma into me regularly got beyond the point in my mind at which I could function as a clinician, i.e. use a mental consulting room in which to think about my experience or at least a waiting room in which I could sit reasonably comfortably with my thoughts until they became clearer. Once he had got past this point in my mind and into my personal space, in which I tend to turn a blind eye to provocation up to a point and beyond this to react aggressively, it was almost inevitable that I would enact my difficulty. I took great care not to do this but would then find that this was not just a proper attempt to maintain a professional stance but in itself a manifestation of the patient's projection, which had found its place in my personality, of a kind of emotional timidity. Thus there were times when my interpretations either avoided the live rail or touched it dangerously. In the latter times my interpretations could have an attacking and sometimes snide quality. Most frequently I would only recognise this by noting his response to what I had said, although sometimes I would be able to see myself that my tone of voice or the way I had worded my interpretation had betrayed my anger or irritation.

Over time, as I continued to think through my countertransferential feelings, I was able to find ways of talking to him about the position he put me in and the way that it paralleled his own. I would interpret that by these means he was communicating to me both his sense of being robbed and his difficulty in experiencing it in a thinkable way that would enable him to communicate it by putting it into words. This period of work undoubtedly helped the patient become more communicative and spontaneous and I noted a greater ability to bring his dreams to the analysis.

The analysis ended prematurely after three years because of my decision to move away from London. However, the progress that had been made in that time enabled him to speak much more freely about his feelings including, of course, his sense that he was being robbed by the termination of his analysis. Poignantly and movingly he was able at times to link this to a sense that he had been robbed of the experience of having had a normal upbringing with normal parents. After his treatment with me finished he had another long analysis with a colleague.

Discussion

Mr C's case is one which could be called a character analysis in that most areas of his life and functioning were beset by harsh restrictions. Like at the meal times in his family, at any moment he could be accused of doing something wrongly. The way that this had pervaded his character and made him regard others as wrong-doers is also indicated. It took a considerable length of time for this to be experienced fully in the analysis and had to be worked through in the countertransference before it could be synthesised and symbolically depicted in a dream. In Bion's (1962) terms the patient was unable to apply alpha function to a beta element, for example, a gut feeling of having been robbed of a fundamental right. The element was then felt to be fit only for evacuation via enactment or projection. The analyst too received this experience as a beta element and his first reaction was also to want to be rid of it. In Mr C's case this involved ignoring the sense of feeling bored and robbed by him. In Mr B's case the great discomfort caused by the projection might have resulted in quickly saying: "In these extraordinary circumstances, of course I won't charge you for the session".

In order to be able to engage with these difficulties psychoanalytically, the analyst must have available to him the capacity to consult with himself and to tolerate waiting in uncertainty until he can think through what is going on, as my dream about Mr B demonstrates. This is not possible in very many cases and the analyst will unconsciously rid himself of discomforting beta elements before he has been able to apply a psychoanalytic function to them. It can be argued that a primary aim of psychoanalysis, the issue with which I began this chapter, is to enable the psychoanalytic function in the patient. To be able to confront difficult aspects of external and internal reality and to be able to bear them emotionally (for example loss and the feelings it evokes), are the hallmarks of a healthy mind, from a psychoanalytic perspective at least.

One reality that has to be faced is that the achievements of an analytic treatment are both modest and commonplace. For all the hard work that the patients and I put into their treatments, what was achieved was that I helped these two men deal with life a little bit better. How ordinary these achievements might seem: Mr C was helped to know that he had strong feelings about the misfortunes fate had dealt him, including having an analyst who chose to move to another part of the country. Mr B was helped to face the realities of life: that loss was inevitable and had to be suffered and that at times this seemed disproportionate and very unfair, as when his analyst charged for missed sessions.

When I first published the account of Mr B's analysis together with a report of the treatment of Mr C, I used both cases to illustrate the use of dream space and the importance of dreaming, in its widest sense, in working through in the patient and in the analyst (Sedlak, 1997). I have since come to realise that a deeper and related matter was at issue in both analyses: essentially the difficulty in knowing and bearing the knowledge one gains about oneself and one's objects, due to the strictures on thought and perception imposed by a pathological superego. As I have illustrated, this difficulty will be experienced by the analyst too. This is what Brenman Pick (2012) had in mind when she wrote:

> the patient does not just project into the analyst but instead patients are skilled at projecting into particular aspects of the analyst's mind ... into his instinctual sadism, or into his defences against this .... [A]bove all he or she projects into the analyst's guilt, or into the analyst's internal objects .... And they, patients, may be very astute at "reading" how the analyst copes ... or not.

Bion (1965, p. 64) argued that an essential quality of beta elements "is the moral component" which is "inseparable from guilt and responsibility and from a sense that the link between one object ... and another ... is moral causation". Since by definition beta elements are elements that cannot be worked through in order to then be represented by thoughts, Bion was stating that the major impediment to scientific thought (that is, in the analyst's case, clinical thought) is the preponderance of moral associations. Hence, if one does not rid oneself of the beta element there follows a period of personal discomfort that can be very acute, as was mine with Mr B as he argued about the awfulness of my charging him. Over time there is then some growing recognition that the nature of the discomfort has some analytic meaning connected to the patient. In such a situation this always seems to follow later and is dependent, I will argue, on the analyst's relationship with his own superego, or rather as the next chapter will convey, superegos.

2

THE PSYCHOANALYST'S SUPEREGOS

Introduction

John Steiner (2013), speaking of his experiences as Hanna Segal's patient at her memorial meeting in London, said that Segal thought that Freud had created a setting "where kindness and support could be provided in a manner which retained the analyst's objectivity and which kept the search for truth as a guiding principle". She believed that kindness and support were "essential in moderating the harshness which truth can sometimes evoke". Steiner then added:

> I think Hanna Segal's kindness was accompanied by a respect for truth and indeed her kindness made truth more acceptable and less persecuting …. [T]ruth without kindness is not really true, but we would add that kindness without truth is not really kind.

These statements suggest that the analyst will need to find a way of speaking to the patient about difficult and painful matters without being harsh and that this may be problematic. Steiner also implied that the analyst may evade the speaking of difficult truths in order not to be experienced as harsh and that this will in effect short-change the patient. These matters relate not only to tact as an analytic function (Poland, 1975) but also, I will argue, to the analyst's relationship to his superego. The various ways of conceptualising the superego, its genesis and its functions are the subject of this chapter.

Strachey (1934) in his paper on the therapeutic action of psychoanalytic treatment argued that when psychoanalysis is helpful it is because the patient's superego is modified. This then allows for a) a more accepting relationship to oneself and, in consequence,

31

b) a greater awareness of one's propensity to transfer perceptions, thoughts and emotions from one's history onto "new" situations and people. I will argue that when Strachey wrote his famous and influential paper he was not sufficiently aware of the difficulties that this process posed for the analyst.

The superego concept

The superego as a psychoanalytic concept is recognised and used by psychoanalysts of all schools. It is an integral part of an understanding of the dynamic unconscious mind and of the fundamental issue of conflict. Sandler and Sandler (1987) observed that in Britain, where object relations theory has become the paradigm of choice, "[t]he concept of superego as a large-scale structure or agency is probably ... found less useful than the concept of internal object relations" (p. 331). However, in everyday clinical discussions and in significant theoretical contributions from all three groups in the British Society (e.g. Malcolm, 1988; O'Shaughnessy, 1999; Symington, 2007; and Joseph Sandler himself, 1960) the concept of the superego is regularly employed. Malcolm (1988) stated that "the superego *is* the internal objects" (p. 159, original italics). This view is probably too all-encompassing to be useful; it may be more advantageous to consider the use of the concept as a form of shorthand to denote important nuclei of certain kinds of object relations: those pertaining to moral judgement, whether that be sadistic and draconian, or reasonable and supportive.

A selective review of the literature on the superego follows; it is largely limited to a consideration of the views of American-based ego psychologists and the Kleinian literature. The aim is not to offer a comprehensive review but rather to highlight the complexity of the concept, particularly the differing views on the superego's origins and its role in both clinical pathology and everyday wellbeing. As with other similar conceptual divergence, all proponents can cite Freud as a supportive source for their views. Some authors have argued that this is because Freud mistakenly broadened his views on the superego to include erroneous conceptualisation (for example, Gray, 1987, see below). However, it can also be contended that this reflected Freud's sophisticated ability to sustain conflicting perspectives if the clinical evidence merited an overdetermined and complex formulation.

One complication stems from the fact that Freud considered the superego to be a *model* to which the ego aspired (initially called the ego ideal) and also a *function* of observation and judgement. In his most comprehensive discussion of the superego and its formation and function (Freud, 1923), he regularly used the terms superego and ego ideal interchangeably (for example, "a differentiation within the ego, which may be called the 'ego ideal' or 'superego'" p. 28). After 1923 he used the term ego ideal only occasionally. In this book the one term superego will be used except in instances where an aspirational model is the issue – then the term ego ideal will be used.

The superego as the heir to the Oedipus complex

For the purpose of exposition Freud's dating of the formation of the superego to the working through of the Oedipal situation and the ways that the ego psychologists developed this further will be considered first. In short, Freud hypothesised that the little boy formed, in parallel, an object cathexis to his mother and an identification with his father who he took as a model. Then because of "the irresistible advance towards a unification of mental life" (Freud, 1921, p. 105) these two collide, so to speak, and the boy sees that his father stands in the way to his mother: the Oedipus complex. The working through of this, involving having to renounce the possession of desired objects, was the means by which the superego was formed. In this way the superego was the heir to the Oedipus complex; as possession of the external objects was renounced so they were internalised but, in this respect, as authoritarian figures: "As the child was once under a compulsion to obey its parents, so the ego submits to the categorical imperative of its superego" (Freud, 1923, p. 48).

It was primarily among the United States-based ego psychologists that the view that the superego is most usefully conceptualised as a differentiation or a modification of the ego, made necessary by conflicts stimulated by the Oedipal situation, was developed. Hartmann et al. (1946) firmly placed superego development at the age of three/four/five years when the child reaches the phallic stage (they confined their paper to a consideration of the male child). They hypothesised that at that time the boy becomes more aware of his sexual excitement and desire for incestuous objects, and therefore there is a corresponding anxiety about being punished for these wishes and/or masturbatory activities. They described the twin fears of castration and the loss of the father, who outside the area of conflict is loved and whose loss is feared, as is the loss of love from both parents for disobeying their strictures against masturbation. They referred to an earlier paper by Hartmann and Kris (1945) in which it was argued that the fear of castration is in effect not primary but based on earlier fears of losing the love of the parents (thus conceptually implying that in girls the same kind of dynamic development will occur, although they do not draw out this implication). They followed Freud in arguing that the child, in an attempt to safeguard himself against the dangers incited by his sexual wishes, identified himself with the superego of the parents i.e. with those aspects of his parents that forbid masturbation. They also stated that this is a different form of idealisation from that which previously aggrandised the parents in order to feel protected by supreme beings; this later Oedipal idealisation is of moral strictures. They concurred with Freud that once the superego is established the perceived danger that the ego has to guard against is not punishment from the parents but accusations from the superego that induce guilt and shame.

Brenner (1982), while mainly following Hartmann et al. (1946) considerably amplified the role of libido in the formation of the superego (without denying the importance of aggression). Like Hartmann et al. he viewed the superego as a compromise formation, formed by conflict which then itself comes to play a fundamental part in subsequent conflicts: "among the many compromise formations which result from oedipal conflicts, the ones which have to do with morality make up the superego. ... [T]hey persist throughout life. It is they which form the basis of the moral aspect of psychic functioning" (1982, p. 504). For Brenner too the moral inhibitions come first from the outside and begin at the stage of toilet training: "For a young child morality means essentially feeling, thinking and behaving in such a way as to avoid the calamity of being punished" (p. 504). As well as the fear of loss of love Brenner also underlined the role of masochism in the formation of the superego – i.e. it is not just formed in order to forestall punishment by appeasing the parents; it also satisfies the boy's wishes to be loved as a girl. (This formulation depends on a particular meaning of masochism and might more appropriately be considered as a wish to be receptive or passive as opposed to active.)

34

An important part of the contribution of the ego psychologists is their stress on Freud's understanding that the superego is not formed only as a defence against aggression and concomitant fear in the Oedipal period but that it is also established on the basis of love. There are references to this in Freud (1939), and they are important since they underline the crucial role of the superego in mental health rather than pathology. Thus Freud wrote: "When the ego has brought the super-ego the sacrifice of an instinctual renunciation, it expects to be rewarded by receiving more love from it. The consciousness of deserving this love is felt by it as pride." Just a little later he indicated a developmentally earlier version of this process:

> At the time when the authority had not yet been internalized as a super-ego, there could be the same relation between the threat of loss of love and the claims of instinct: there was a feeling of security and satisfaction when one had achieved an instinctual renunciation *out of love for one's parents.*
>
> (Freud, p. 117, italics added)

In this passage Freud indicated a process which is essentially a submission to parental authority but more predicated on love rather than hate and fear, not only the wish for love, but also because of the love for the parents and the child's wishes to please them. It can be argued that this is a renunciation that involves a more mature ambivalence to the parents – for instance, the boy conceding the mother to the father because his competitive animosity is tempered by his love.

Two papers, both published in 1960 although independently (A.-M. Sandler, personal communication) argued that there was a danger that the loving and supportive aspects of the superego, which the ego psychologists had stressed, were in danger of being disregarded by psychoanalysts. In a very careful and comprehensive review of all of Freud's writing on the superego Schafer (1960) gave a number of instances in which Freud was clearly aware of a more benign and supportive superego, although he (Freud) frequently situated this kind of superego as being part of the ego. Sandler (also 1960), as part of his study of the use of the Hampstead Index, noted that clinicians would often assign abilities to make appropriate moral judgements and to provide moral support and guidance to the self in times of stress, to the ego. He argued for the recognition of these functions as residing in the superego. Like Schafer, Sandler stressed that these functions give the ego a sense of being loveable and they support it when it feels under pressure; both authors argued that this function of the superego is essential to mental health and should be recognised as being separate from the ego.

In explaining the harsh severity of the superego the ego psychologists considered that it is principally due to the strength of the child's Oedipal "incestuous, murderous, sadomasochistic wishes" (Brenner, 1982, p. 505). Thus while narcissistic wishes, frustration and aggression, are clearly indicated in this formulation, the emphasis is on the Oedipal origins and experience of these.

The death instinct and Klein's views on the superego

One striking feature of the ego psychologists' views is their relative disregard of another hypothesis about the development of the superego which is described in Freud's 1923 contribution: that of the influence of the death instinct. Indeed both Brenner (1982) and Gray (1987) argued that Freud's elevation of aggression to the status of a drive was a mistake on Freud's part and diverted analytic attention away from analysis of the superego. Gray also argued that the introduction of the death instinct implied that some clinical problems were to be seen as intractable. (Frank, 2015, also noted this response in some European analytic circles.) This pessimism is not reflected in Freud's modest but not completely despairing view when he wrote of interpreting unconscious guilt in the severe neuroses: "In warding off this resistance we are obliged to restrict ourselves to making it conscious and attempting to bring about the slow demolition of the hostile super-ego" (Freud, 1938, p. 180).

In *The Ego and the Id* (1923), having acknowledged one foundation for the superego to be an identification with the parents' superego, Freud turned to his clinical observations of the negative therapeutic reaction, obsessive-compulsive disorders and melancholia, and he reminded the reader of the concept of the death instinct that he had introduced in 1920. To my mind Freud's discomfort with this is evident in the text: having introduced the death instinct he kept going back to the Oedipal origins of superego formation, then to a different genesis (not considered in this review and not taken up by many commentators – the phylogenetic component) and then back again to the death instinct. Frank (2015, p. 427) has noted a similar "hesitancy" in Freud's writing about the death instinct in *Beyond the Pleasure Principle*. Gray (1987, p. 136) cited a number of communications in the 1930s in which Freud indicated that he continued to doubt that he had been correct in introducing the death instinct as a primary drive. While Freud was uncomfortable with the concept of the death instinct, clinical phenomena in which he had experienced the presence of something really destructive and potentially intractable, kept bringing him back to the idea that the source of such aggression must be of an archaic and primordial nature.

Freud's concept of the death instinct or death drive was essentially a biological one, but those who took it up and used it theoretically conceptualised its functioning in psychological terms (Bell, 2015; Frank, 2015). Segal (1993, p. 55) put it most clearly when she wrote:

Birth confronts us with the experience of needs. In relation to that experience there can be two reactions, and both, I think, are invariably present in all of us, though in varying proportions. One, to seek satisfaction for the needs: that is life-promoting and leads to object seeking, love, and eventually object concern. The other is the drive to annihilate the need, to annihilate the perceiving experiencing self, as well as anything that is perceived.

It is this way of seeing the death instinct which has been found most useful: as a psychological force which reacts with destructiveness when the ego is confronted with frustration, and it is this definition that I will use in this book. It is interesting to see how close Freud appeared to be to this psychological formulation even as he was developing the concept of a biological drive: "The emergence of life would thus be the continuance of the cause of life and also at the same time of the striving towards death" (1923, pp. 40–41). And a little later in the same text (p. 42): "For the opposition of the two classes of instincts we may put the polarity of love and hate."

In my view the elemental force which has been called the death instinct is a potential at birth. It is perhaps akin to Bion's idea of a preconception which, when it mates with a realisation, becomes a conception; the hatred and outrage and instinctual destructiveness are a potential but they have to mate with the realisation of a frustration in order to be activated. I would add that it always

37

remains as a potential in the individual and can erupt at times of great stress and frustration, experiences I will argue that are not uncommon to the practising analyst.

It is the death instinct as a psychological phenomenon which is implicated in the Klein's view of the development of the superego. Like Freud, Klein came to her views on the basis of clinical experience:

> When at the beginning of the twenties I embarked on the new ven-
> ture of analysing by play technique children from their third year
> onwards, one of the unexpected phenomena I came across was
> a very early and savage super-ego. I also found that young children
> introject their parents – first of all the mother and her breast – in
> a phantastic way, and I was led to this conclusion by observing the
> terrifying character of some of their internalized objects.
>
> (Klein, 1958, p. 241)

Klein not only located the Oedipus complex at a much earlier stage in life than did Freud, but she also thought that the dynamics which resulted in the creation of the superego began at birth with the conflict between the life and death instincts (Klein, 1958, p. 239). Both Freud and Klein recognised that the infant or young child would be subject to frustration (Oedipal or in the earliest mother–infant interaction), and that this would evoke aggressive and destructive feelings which would in turn be projected and hence cause anxiety in the form of a dread of retaliation. The process of projection and subsequent introjection would create terrifying internal objects and come to form the basis of the cruel superego. In stressing the destructive impulses and their psychic consequences Klein was close to Freud's view of the formation of the censorious superego although she hypothesised that the dating of this was much earlier than that usually considered by Freud. Although, as Klein (1948) notes:

> As regards guilt, Freud held that it has its origin in the Oedipus
> complex and arises as a sequel to it. There are passages, however,
> in which Freud clearly referred to conflict and guilt arising at
> a much earlier stage of life. He wrote: "... guilt is the expression
> of the conflict of ambivalence, *the eternal struggle between Eros and
> the destructive or death instinct*". Also: "... an intensification of the

sense of guilt – resulting from the *innate conflict of ambivalence*, from the eternal struggle between love and the death trends".

(p. 114, Klein's italics throughout)

Klein also greatly amplified the role of love in the formation of the superego and its essential role in psychological wellbeing. She considered that the creation of the good object was in the first instance dependent on the infant's love which was projected into the breast and created the sense of a good breast. Thereafter, if the caretaker was capable of providing good enough care, love was able to balance hate and destructiveness:

> The super-ego ... acquires both protective and threatening qualities .... As the process of integration ... goes on ... the superego – being bound up with the good object and even striving for its preservation – comes close to the actual good mother who feeds the child and takes care of it. ... [S]ince the super-ego is also under the influence of the death instinct, it partly becomes the representative of the mother who frustrates the child, and its prohibitions and accusations arouse anxiety .... Therefore the super-ego is normally established in close relation with the ego and shares different aspects of the same good object. This makes it possible for the ego to integrate and accept the super-ego to a greater or less extent.

(Klein, 1958, p. 241)

One can see in this last statement the move noted by both Schafer (1960) and Sandler (1960) of locating the more benign aspects of the superego in the ego.

Central to Klein's formulation of the less severe superego was the concept of the depressive position. As splitting diminishes (Freud's "irresistible advance towards a unification of mental life", 1921, p. 105), the child becomes more aware that its hatred and its love are directed at the same object. A number of concomitant and concurrent processes occur: love mobilises concern and a wish to repair the internal object which has been damaged by hate; the object, because it is loved and cared for, becomes a less persecutory figure; as an internal object which is less persecutory it is more able to consider and support the ego when personal responsibility for damage has to be considered; as a less persecutory figure the object "approximate[s] more to the real parents; the ego gradually

39

develops its essential function of dealing with the external world" (Klein, 1958, pp. 240–242).

It would appear that Klein conceptualised a development of the superego in which its most terrifying aspects are modified, and it thus becomes capable of a more benign and realistic moral judgement, hence its location, in part, in the ego. However, she also wrote:

> the extremely bad figures are not accepted by the ego in this way and are constantly rejected by it. These extremely dangerous objects give rise, in early infancy, to conflict and anxiety within the ego; but under the stress of acute anxiety they, and other terrifying figures, are split off in a manner *different from that by which the super-ego is formed*, and are relegated to the deeper layers of the unconscious.
>
> (1958, p. 241, italics added)

Klein clarified that these terrifying objects continue to exist by virtue of the fact that their destructiveness is not modified by a fusion with love; they are a product of a failure of that process and demonstrate that there is a part of the mind in which "defusion seems to be in the ascendant" (p. 241).

O'Shaughnessy (1975, pp. 331–332) commented on this passage:

> Here Melanie Klein has a sudden change of view. In contrast to emphatic earlier views ... that the hallmark of the normal early super-ego is its extreme and terrifying nature, she here suggests that the super-ego develops with the two instincts predominantly in a state of fusion, and that the terrifying internal figures which result from intense destructiveness do not form part of the super-ego. These exist in a separate area of the mind in the deep unconscious, split off both from the ego and the super-ego, where they remain unintegrated and unmodified by normal processes of growth; if an abnormal situation arises and there is a failure to maintain a split these terrifying objects become a source of acute anxiety and a threat to mental stability.

The complexity of the superego concept

This necessarily brief and selective review of the American and British literature is intended to illustrate the complexity and potential confusion of the superego concept. It shows important differences between contributors about how the superego is formed, the dating of this and also about its functions. It demonstrates how psychoanalysts, including Freud himself, split off certain functions which were traditionally considered to be located in the superego and located them elsewhere in the tripartite model of the mind. This occurred to the very persecutory aspects of superego functioning (as in Klein in 1958, see above) and also the the benign and supportive ones (the development noted by both Schafer and Sandler, as above). Britton (2003) and Caper (1999) have also argued that the function of considered moral judgement should be assigned to the ego.

Due to these different and sometimes contradictory formulations it is necessary to be relatively precise about the formulation of the superego that is being used. This book follows a number of previous authors, from both sides of the Atlantic, who have distinguished a normal or mature superego from a more primitive and pathological structure (e.g. Grotstein, 2004; Jacobson, 1946; Kramer, 1958; O'Shaughnessy, 1999). Other authors such as Brenman (2006) have referred to a "good object" to mean a normal superego, as did Strachey in his famous paper (1934, p. 139).

The normal and the pathological superegos

The normal superego can be distinguished from the pathological superego in the following ways: it is concerned with nuanced moral judgement which takes reality and humane consideration into account, rather than delivering absolute moralistic condemnation. The normal superego has a developmental trajectory, based on the emotional working through of the renunciation of objects and their attributes; it is essentially a manifestation of the reality principle rather than of the pleasure principle or the death instinct. It is a product of the emotional working through of a clash between a narcissistic insistence that reality should accommodate to the will of the individual and an appreciation, based in part on love of the object, that this is destructive of the object, i.e. it can also be thought to be a product of depressive position functioning.

Unlike the pathological superego, the normal superego continues to develop throughout life into middle and old age as narcissistic injuries are encountered and worked through. Ingham (2007) provided a convincing example of the development of a normal superego in youth and young adulthood, and the link with the development from pathological to healthy narcissism, by analysing Dickens' portrayal of the character of Pip in *Great Expectations*.

The development of the normal superego does not mean that the pathological superego ceases to exist; it continues to be a potential regressive possibility at times of stress, particularly in reaction to narcissistic injury and frustration. When Freud wrote of the difficulty of mourning a lost object he stated that "it is a matter of general observation that people never willingly abandon a libidinal position …. This opposition can be so intense that a turning away from reality takes place" (Freud, 1917a, p. 244). Freud's observation also implies that the reaction to repudiate reality is also never totally nor permanently abandoned and remains a potential.

It is beyond the scope of this book to review comprehensively the literature on the link between primitive or pathological narcissism and a pathological superego. Ingham's paper (2007) does this using literary evidence, and Kernberg (1974) has provided the most clinically precise descriptions of this link, stressing for instance the unintegrated and hence ambivalently aggressive nature of the superego in some forms of narcissistic disorder.

In order to give some indication of the connection between an early form of narcissism and a severe superego and also to illustrate its ubiquity even in relatively sophisticated people Poland's (2009) analysis of why psychoanalysts find it so difficult to learn from other psychoanalytic schools can be considered. Without directly implicating the superego he described dynamics whereby analysts' pathological narcissism, and the consequent inability to accept limitations in understanding, leads to harsh and dismissive assessment of others' viewpoints. The dynamics he described are probably witnessed in all psychoanalytic societies. To give an example: the British Psychoanalytical Society's scientific meetings are at their best when there is a recognition of the difficulties of psychoanalytic work, when there is a thoughtful acknowledgement of the fact of overdetermination in psychic functioning (Gabbard, 2007) so that no one means of understanding a problem is conclusive. The conservatism of the basic material encountered in the work, namely human character, is recognised and personal limitations and the limitations of the psychoanalytic endeavour are accepted. But at times this breaks down and then a different dynamic supplants the co-operative, mutually respectful one which is governed by the aims of scientific curiosity and discovery – the group becomes instead one in which there has to be an *über* and an *unter* (O'Shaughnessy, personal communication). Rather than people feeling supported by a normal superego, tolerant of their limitations, the pathological superego makes its presence felt and then the use of splitting and the projection of unwanted parts of the self into others, where they can be treated with some contempt, is to the fore.

In his paper Poland stated that the difficulty that psychoanalysts sometimes have in listening to their colleagues is not paralleled in their listening to their patients, but I do not agree with this. Clinical contact with patients very often arouses narcissistic concern in the analyst about clinical competence, and then the same dynamics as Poland described in inter-collegial difficulties can occur, as I will illustrate in the next chapter.

To make one further point about the pathological and the normal superego: a seemingly draconian superego can perversely serve the function of protecting the patient from depressive pain. I have treated patients who were lacerating in their criticisms of themselves and who regularly threatened suicide but in so doing they seemed to evade a potentially far more dangerous despair which would come from a less excited and more realistic appraisal of how they had led their lives and formed their relationships. The normal superego is not a soft touch, it can be appropriately critical and this can lead to enormous pain and suffering which can at times be experienced as unbearable. Two patients in particular come to mind: both employed as a main form of defence an excited self-condemnation which was perverse and sado-masochistic, not only in their treatment of themselves but also of their analyst. Both analyses broke down after about a year when the patient appeared to be threatened by a more realistic and sober judgement about what they were doing and had done for much of their lives. At that point real despair arose, which did actually feel dangerous in terms of suicide risk; this was the point at which both patients chose to leave their analysis. One of these treatments is described in Chapter 5.

Patients who avoid a serious examination of their actual situation and their part in it by an excited relationship with a pathological superego are particularly difficult to treat since they can also be extremely skilled in drawing the analyst into acting as a pathological superego. However patients who do not primarily employ this defence will also regularly put the analyst's relationship with his superego to the test. For instance patients who suffer from a melancholic guilt will not allow themselves to be helped by the analyst, and this in itself will lead to further guilt, and a vicious circle can be set up in which the analyst is nudged into being critical of the patient and, of course, of himself. But in any treatment the analyst will be regularly confronted with narcissistic disappointment, and how this is contained or enacted may be crucial. As Brenman Pick (2012) stated:

> the patient does not just project into the analyst but instead patients are skilled at projecting into particular aspects of the analyst's mind … into his instinctual sadism, or into his defences against this …. [A]bove all he or she projects into the analyst's guilt, or into the analyst's internal objects. … And they, patients, may be very astute at "reading" how the analyst copes … or not.

A consideration of Strachey's (1934) paper

One theory of psychoanalytic cure is that, after a successful analysis, a person will know themselves better. However in order to attain some measure of wellbeing from a psychoanalytic treatment a further requirement has to be met: this knowledge of oneself has to be *tolerable*.

Strachey (1934) described in detail the crucial role of the superego in the complex relationship between analyst and patient and in relation to the development of self-knowledge. To briefly rehearse Strachey's reasoning: his paper is first and foremost an argument for the need to address "the point of urgency", that is, the *current* emotional situation in the analytic relationship; in this sense the paper is very much in keeping with a contemporary approach. He wrote:

> Instead of having to deal as best we may with conflicts of the remote past, which are concerned with dead circumstances and mummified personalities, and whose outcome is already determined, we find ourselves involved in an actual and immediate situation, in which we and the patient are the principal characters.
>
> (p. 132)

And:

> Since the analyst is also, from the nature of things, the object of the patient's id-impulses, the quantity of these impulses which is

now released into consciousness will become consciously directed towards the analyst. This is the critical point.

(pp. 142–143)

Strachey went on to argue that in the giving of an interpretation the analyst showed the patient that the critical and harsh judgement that the patient felt towards himself, for example, for harbouring hostile thoughts towards the analyst, could be named and contemplated. The hostility that was repressed and could only emerge in derivative form, which the analyst comprehended, could more openly be owned and, hopefully, form part of a healthily ambivalent relationship to the analyst. Thus the analyst functioned as the patient's auxiliary superego, and the patient was able to internalise, via re-introjection, this more tolerant stance and understand that his expectation of the analyst's harshness was due to his own projection. In this way the patient found out something about himself *and* was able to develop a tolerance of this aspect of himself.

Strachey (p. 146) stressed that:

> the patient is all the time on the brink of turning the real external object (the analyst) into the archaic one; that is to say, he is on the brink of projecting his primitive introjected imagos on to him. The analyst then ceases to possess the peculiar advantages derived from the analytic situation; he will be introjected like all other phantasy objects into the patient's super-ego, and will no longer be able to function in the peculiar ways which are essential to the effecting of a mutative interpretation.

Strachey warned against the analyst trying to show himself as a "good object" and thereby trying to promote a positive transference of the patient's "archaic good objects". He did not believe that this promotion of a positive transference would alter the nature and severity of the patient's "archaic bad objects" (in effect, the patient's archaic or primitive superego).

Until the last page of his paper Strachey gave little indication that maintaining analytic neutrality would pose a difficulty for the analyst, except where he warned against actively trying to show oneself to be a "good" object. However at this late point he introduced another element into his argument. There he made the important observation that:

there is sometimes a lurking difficulty in the actual *giving* [Strachey's italics] of the interpretation, for there seems to be a constant temptation for the analyst to do something else instead. He may ask questions, or he may give reassurances or advice or discourses upon theory, or he may give interpretations – but interpretations that are not mutative, extra-transference interpretations, interpretations that are non-immediate, or ambiguous, or inexact – or he may give two or more alternative interpretations simultaneously, or he may give interpretations and at the same time show his own scepticism about them. All of this strongly suggests that the giving of a mutative interpretation is a crucial act for the analyst as well as for the patient, and that he is exposing himself to some great danger in doing so. And this in turn will become intelligible when we reflect that at the moment of interpretation the analyst is in fact deliberately evoking a quantity of the patient's id-energy while it is alive and actual and unambiguous and aimed directly at himself. Such a moment must above all others put to the test his relations with his own unconscious impulses.

(pp. 158–159)

This last intriguing sentence ends Strachey's paper.

There are at least two different ways of understanding this last part of Strachey's paper. The first reading is straightforward and it is the one that Strachey makes explicit: the analyst fears that the "great danger" is that the interpretation will incite or evoke "a quantity of the patient's id-energy ... aimed directly at himself" (the analyst). A different way of looking at this is to put the greater stress on the last sentence of Strachey's paper: "Such a moment must above all others put to the test his relations with his own unconscious impulses." This throws into question whether Strachey simply meant that the analyst may unconsciously fear the patient's hostility that the interpretation may release; that, while being able to comprehend its unconscious manifestation, the analyst nevertheless fears its undisguised and direct expression. Probably he does not mean this – he explicitly names the *analyst's* impulses; thus it is far more likely that he means that the analyst fears that in giving his interpretation he will unwittingly expose his own hitherto unexpressed and maybe unconscious affective response. If one considers this as the possibility that Strachey is somewhat obliquely hinting at then other parts of his paper can be read differently: for example when Strachey

46

wrote of "the commonly felt fear of the explosive possibilities of interpretation" (p. 150) one can now ask *whose* explosive possibilities? The argumentation radically changes to: the analyst is frightened that in interpreting the current situation he (the analyst) will communicate and direct a quantity of the *analyst's* hostility while it is alive and actual and unambiguous and aimed directly *at the patient*. Of course this will expose the analyst to a danger but it is not, in the first instance, of a confrontation with the patient's hostility, although that may follow. The primary danger is that the analyst will communicate his own hostility while addressing the current situation; the analyst's fear is that he is not able to maintain a professional neutrality in considering the current emotional situation and that this will be betrayed in the manner of speaking the interpretation. The associated anxiety for the analyst is that the judgement of his own superego will then be turned upon him and will accuse the analyst of having damaged the patient by giving voice to his critical superego and thereby reinforcing the hostility of the patient's superego.

This change of stress in reading Strachey's paper brings into focus the analyst's fears that in his interpretation of the patient's aggression the analyst will betray his own hostility; if he does so then he won't be behaving like an auxiliary normal superego but rather as a judgemental harsh one or, perhaps more confusingly, as a harsh superego trying to masquerade as a benign one.

One can argue that, while Strachey was descriptively right in arguing that the patient will project his "archaic" superego onto the analyst, he held back, until the last page of his paper, in clarifying just what a difficult emotional task this will set for the analyst. I think that Strachey was not able to work through the full implications of his observation that the analyst will have a difficulty in giving an interpretation that takes up the immediate issues in the analysis and the reasons for this. He came very close to describing what we would now think of as the analyst's difficulty in managing the countertransference (Brenman Pick, 1985). In the latter part of the paper Strachey mentioned conversations with Klein, and it may be that his understating of this dilemma, which is only hinted at in the last sentence of his paper, was due to Klein's influence. She tended to think that countertransference was a consequence of the analyst's pathology (Spillius, 1994, p. 352). Klein's view was a reflection of the general belief in 1934 that acting-in of the countertransference was an analytic failure, diagnostic of the analyst's need for further analysis. It was not until the publication of Heimann's (1950) paper that consideration of the countertransference, and an acknowledgement that its partial enactment was inevitable and could be subsequently clinically informative, became an accepted wisdom.

This way of looking at Strachey's paper suggests at least one important aspect of what he called in his last sentence "the analyst's relation with his unconscious impulses". Strachey indicated that the analyst will be anxious that he will not be able to convey convincingly that his impulse is governed by a normal superego; he will be anxious that his choice of words or his tone or some other non-verbal way of communicating will betray that the interpretation is intended as a criticism or as a punishment, that is to say, an expression of his pathological superego.

Two clinical vignettes

A female patient occasionally had to cancel sessions due to having to accompany her husband to important social gatherings connected with his work; sometimes these involved nationally and internationally known figures from the worlds of politics and entertainment. It was difficult for the analyst to interpret with conviction that the patient was using these imposing realities to diminish the importance of her analyst and analysis. Indeed he sometimes found himself thinking that it would be revealing of his own wounded narcissism to suggest that she might even consider missing an opportunity to meet a very well-known personality with her husband in order to attend her analytic session.

One day, following another cancelled session to attend a particularly prestigious gala, the patient described that as she and her husband had walked up the red carpet to the foyer of the grand hotel where the gala was being held, someone from the crowd of onlookers had vaulted a barrier and made towards her and her husband in a threatening way. The intruder had been roughly wrestled to the floor by stewards and then marched off. She described this person as poorly nourished and badly dressed and thought that he might have been involved in a protest against inequality. This was soon after the economic crash of 2008 when such protests were receiving a lot of publicity.

The analyst quickly realised the transferential meaning of this and prepared to describe how the patient, by absenting herself from her sessions, did put him in the position of an onlooker who was made to feel deprived and hence attacking. However, he was sufficiently aware of his wish to make *immediate* use of this thought, and in particular to elaborate upon the inequality between them that her husband's status gave her and the use she made of this, to be able to take note of this sense of urgency. He was able to hold the thought and further consideration made it clear that he had been harbouring hostile feelings about the way she had used the reality of her commitment to accompany her husband as a means of upstaging her analyst.

A few sessions later there was another opportunity to interpret to the patient about the way that she upstaged the analyst, but by this time the analyst was in a more considered state of mind and more able to regard the patient's behaviour as her right as a patient – that is, the right to bring to her analysis her habitual ways of relating. The patient was uncomfortable in considering this aspect of her behaviour, but in the subsequent period of analysis it became possible for her to think about the ways that she could make others feel her inferior, and about her own anxiety about being made to feel second rate. In a session a few days after the analyst had taken up her treatment of him, the patient told of how she had been able to talk to her husband about her hurt and anger about a longstanding problem between them. Previously she had been frightened to talk to him about this because she feared that her hostility would lead her to attack him. It is probable that the patient sensed the analyst's tolerating of and working through of the countertransference, particularly the outlined struggle with his critical superego, and this was helpful to her in the manner suggested by Carpy (1989).

This is not primarily, or entirely, an example of an analyst being able to contain and work through the countertransference, and having done so, being able to give a mutative interpretation. In the period during which the patient was cancelling sessions without this being interpreted, the analyst was acting in the way that Strachey described in the last part of his paper: "there is sometimes a lurking difficulty in the actual giving of the interpretation". Unconsciously the analyst (and the patient) sensed that if he were to vault the (internal) barrier and approach her while he was feeling badly treated then he would be threatening her with accusation. Hence he kept himself behind the barrier and yet, in the way that a defence carries the germ of the thing defended against, he was punishing her by depriving her of a means of getting to know herself better. In this sense he was not containing but enacting. This also illustrates that while he struggled with his wounded narcissism the analyst was unable to treat himself kindly and gain the support of his normal superego which would have commiserated with his pain and might have supported him better in tolerating the feeling of emasculation. Such a normal superego might also have been more tolerant of his wish to be the chosen man and part of the Oedipal couple without then accusing him of the unprofessional behaviour of essentially intending to surpass the patient's husband in her affections.

Very frequently this kind of scenario does lead to the analyst interpreting with some implied criticism and then the consequences of this, with the patient feeling admonished, having to be worked through. This is a regular aspect of many if not all analyses; even when a direct enactment is avoided, some expression of the analyst's unconscious attitude is still subtly enacted, either by commission or omission. It is somewhat outside the scope of this chapter but it is worth noting that the way that the analyst eventually deals with this sort of situation will be comprehended by the patient, consciously or unconsciously, and will be experienced by both analyst and patient as an aspect of the analyst's reparative efforts.

An example of an analyst being able to pay heed to the dynamics of superego enactment is given in O'Shaughnessy's (1999) paper. She had been able to describe to a patient, Mr B, the way that he had destroyed contact between them towards the end of a session before a long weekend break. He had done so by fantasising about a "girlie house" − a kind of brothel to which men had an exclusive key; in that session he had gone on to imagine what his analyst would look like if he undressed her. When he returned to the next session he was in despair and completely hopeless about the possibility of improvement. He reported a dream in which there was a book entitled *Sceptic of the Renaissance*. O'Shaughnessy interpreted to him that he was sure that *she* was sceptical about *him*. Interestingly, at that point in the session, the patient had forgotten that the issue of scepticism had been indicated in his dream: probably a measure of how comprehensively he had

50

projected this quality into his view of his analyst. She related his expectation of her scepticism to the previous session when:

> his undressing fantasies destroyed our analytic work. When I named his actual crime his terror and despair left him, and instead of being a Sceptic I became a normal superego who called things by their proper names – a normal superego, but one with an analytic attitude. This means not giving verdicts … but recognising things for what they are in the ethical domain. Mr B then knows a named crime for which he himself may (if he is able to) feel guilt instead of near-psychotic panic. In my view, because of the antagonism between the pathological super-ego and the operation of normal ethics, escaping its clutches and regaining contact with an object with normal superego aspects are among the more significant analytic events in clinical work with patients.
>
> (p. 869)

In this example the analyst directly addressed the patient's anticipation of her superego. She was aware that the patient's initial concern was with the analyst's moral judgement of what he had done. It would have been easy but clinically ineffectual to interpret that the patient was himself sceptical about his ability to repair the damage he phantasised he had done. Indeed, had she interpreted in this way it is likely that the patient would have heard her as being sceptical of his reparative capacity but, having been unable to think about and own this scepticism, she had instead enacted it in her interpretation and accused him of scepticism. In this clinical situation the analyst must have done some very important internal work in which there would have been an awareness of the possibility of behaving as a pathological superego; this awareness enabled her to make her telling interpretation.

Very frequently the analyst is unable, under the strain of the clinical situation, to be able to realise what the actual dynamics in a clinical encounter are. Klein (1948; footnote, p. 122) wrote:

> If a normal person is put under a severe internal or external strain, or if he falls ill or fails in some other way, we may observe in him the full and complete operation of his deepest

anxiety-situations … it follows that he can never have entirely given up his old anxiety-situations.

This is as true of the analyst as it is of other people, and hence the analyst too is faced with the possibility of regressing to his original ways of dealing with anxiety situations. The next chapter explores this difficulty in greater detail.

3

FROM DREAD TO ANXIETY

Introduction

When I was a candidate in training a senior colleague told me that, when he looked back on his clinical experience of completed analyses, he could divide them into two main groups: those which he recalled as having had a central issue which had encapsulated the patient's core difficulty, and those which had meandered along until they reached an ending without a central theme having emerged. Reflecting on my own experience I find myself adding a third category: those analyses in which a central issue did not emerge, but which with hindsight I later judged to have contained a pivotal difficulty which the patient and I colluded in avoiding. An example comes readily to mind: a patient who, when faced with a difficulty, would arrive at a somewhat easy resolution, without there having been a convincing sense of struggle and suffering. On reaching such a resolution he would declare a renewed confidence in the usefulness of his analysis. This constellation, of an agreement between analyst and patient that the treatment is proceeding satisfactorily, whilst at the same time there is an undefined but lurking sense that nothing very substantial is actually taking place, is the most common example of the problem I want to address. In such cases it seems that there is a dread of contemplating the possibility that the analysis, or indeed any other relationship to which the patient may turn to, will ultimately be experienced as futile. The dread about bringing this situation out into the open means that the dynamics which lead to such an impasse remain unexplored.

A supervisee discussed a case with me in which he disclosed that he felt his work was somewhat superficial and that, while it looked all right from a passing glance, a more searching look would reveal it to be shallow or hollow. The session he presented came from a week in which there had been a public holiday and towards the end of the session the patient had said "I am very afraid that you think me to be shallow and that my talk is of little consequence". In response the analyst took up the missing session and the patient's anxiety that it was having an effect on the depth at which they were able to work that week. What was striking to me however was how accurately the patient had diagnosed the problem in the analysis, which was of much greater significance and duration than simply pertaining to that week, and that the analyst had in effect stopped this line of thought. I should say that the analyst is an experienced colleague whose work I trust. When I look back at those terminated cases of mine in which I experienced a growing sense that something crucial was not allowed to materialise sufficiently, I am surprised and feel somewhat ashamed that such a blind spot persisted throughout the analysis. I also find myself rather quickly reassuring myself that nevertheless some good work was done and that both the patient and I came to think that the analysis could be brought to a more or less satisfactory close. That is to say, the situation I want to discuss is not one which would ordinarily be labelled as a "failed analysis".

It is a very common experience for clinicians to look back at cases they have treated and feel guilt about the problems the patient had been left to struggle with on his own after the treatment has finished. Indeed there would be something very odd if an analyst did not feel a sense of having failed in some measure in all analyses, but in the cases I want to discuss this sense of failure, with the passage of time, became particularly severe. The conviction grew that a central difficulty had not been analysed at depth and that the breadth of its quiet but insistent influence on the patient's functioning had also been left unattended. I am going to argue that in these cases both analyst and analysand suffer from a sense of dread, which I take to be at the extreme end of the anxiety–dread continuum.

When Freud (1893, p. 302) wrote: "the patient is seized by a dread of becoming too much accustomed to the physician personally, of losing her independence in relation to him, and even of perhaps becoming sexually dependent on him", he did not clarify whether the patient herself would be consciously aware of what she dreaded. Sometimes the expression is used when the dreaded event can be

54

consciously registered and named. For instance, Freud (1898, p. 324) wrote to Fliess that he "now dreaded actively taking up a writing project that he had hitherto been reading around". Freud was at least able to indicate more or less what he dreaded. However, the common expression "I dread to think what would happen if ..." suggests that in dread there can be a resistance to thought or an inability to think. This hints at another manifestation of dread in which whatever it is that is dreaded is not known or named. This is more akin to the experience described by Bion as "nameless dread" (e.g. 1962, p. 96) and which is probably the same kind of experience that Winnicott (1965, p. 86) referred to as archaic ("unthinkable") anxiety and the threat of feeling that one is "falling for ever" with no sense of a holding environment.

Freud (1920, p. 13) wrote that: "There is something about anxiety that protects its subject against fright and so against fright-neuroses." He meant that anxiety can be preparatory and can safeguard in some sense against the unexpected, but if anxiety is not experienced then there can be a dread of being overwhelmed. In the same book (p. 36) he wrote of an "obscure fear − a dread of rousing something that ... is better left sleeping". He suggested that this "something" may be possessed of a "daemonic" power. There is the suggestion that it would take some courage to awaken to a fear and to feel anxiety rather than dread.

Earlier, Freud (1914a, p. 152) had written that the patient:

> must find the courage to direct his attention to the phenomena of his illness. His illness itself must no longer seem to him contemptible, but must become an enemy worthy of his mettle, a piece of his personality, which has solid ground for its existence.

Elsewhere he suggested that there could be a counterpart of this timidity in the analyst too; in considering the analyst's reluctance to analyse the patient's sexualisation of the transference he wrote of "the physician's incapacity to help him to overcome his resistances, or else to the physician's dread of the results of the work" (Freud, 1914b, p. 66). This was part of a polemic against Jung's abandonment of the central importance of sexuality in the aetiology of neurosis. One may nevertheless find a wider application of Freud's diagnosis of the analyst's part in colluding with the patient's avoidance of a confrontation with the reality of an illness and its manifestation in the transference.

I now want to illustrate the analyst's dread of a confrontation with the patient's illness with a clinical example. It occurred in a treatment in which a fortuitous set of events conspired to bring to light an issue which I suspect might have otherwise remained unexamined.

Clinical example: Mrs D

An intelligent and thoughtful female patient, then in her middle thirties, came for treatment because of a general dissatisfaction with her life. She consciously attributed this to the fact that she did not have children; she held her husband responsible for this. He was considerably older than her and this was his third marriage; he already had three grown-up children and had made it clear from the outset of their relationship that he would not want to start a new family. Nevertheless the patient frequently spoke of how disappointed she was by this state of affairs especially when she saw many of her friends beginning families.

When the patient had been about fifteen, her mother had had an affair with a work colleague and had moved out of the family home for about eighteen months. She had subsequently returned but not before the patient had failed important exams which she had been predicted to pass with flying colours. At that time she had also suffered a severe recurrence of eczema which she had had as an infant but which had cleared up in her latency period. She had subsequently recovered from this a few months after her mother's return; it was understood to have been an emotional reaction to what was happening at that time. I gained the impression that her relationship with her mother had never fully recovered; in the analysis she sometimes referred to her mother's affair as evidence of how cruel and unfair life could be and how little thought others gave to her needs. Her mother had died in a car accident when the patient was in her mid-twenties without there having been a true reconciliation.

She had recovered academically from her failures at the time of her mother's absence and had in fact had considerable success, eventually achieving a prominent position in her field. While her professional successes brought her some pleasure, they had also led to another set of difficulties: she frequently complained of how very hard she had to work to maintain her standing, and how frequently she felt that all her efforts were unappreciated by her students and colleagues.

In the first three years or so of her treatment I frequently discussed her in supervision; generally my sense was that important issues were addressed in her treatment. For instance her rivalry with her colleagues and the consequence of her feeling that others were out to do her down, particularly when she was successful, was examined, and there appeared to be an appropriate working through of this and other significant difficulties in the transference. Without one central theme having emerged I was able to feel that we were making steady progress in her analysis and I generally enjoyed my work with her and felt committed to and interested in her treatment.

One day in the sixth year of her analysis, I said: "I am afraid I have to tell you that in a year's time I will be leaving London and that your analysis with me will have to finish then." As can be imagined I said this after a great deal of thought and consultation with my supervisor and other colleagues. It is a very difficult thing to tell any patient such news; in fact she was the last patient I told since I had procrastinated longer with her than with my other patients.

Her immediate reaction was to be silent for a long period and then to ask if this was "right" – it became clearer in the following sessions that she meant that such behaviour might contravene a code of ethics. She spoke about friends who knew a good deal about psychoanalysis and our Society and who had hinted that a complaint to the Ethics Committee about my behaviour might be in order. For a number of sessions she led me to believe that she had enquired into such a possibility. The sessions continued to be very difficult and painful; my anxiety about what would happen to my patient before and after the termination of the analysis was much in my mind. I worried that she might have a depressive breakdown and become unable to function.

Over the next month, while indicating that she had resigned from her inclination to pursue an ethical complaint about me, alongside her expressed concerns that she might break down, she made increasing reference to an endurance sporting event her husband had entered. He was a very keen participant in this sport; his wish to dedicate himself to this and the long training hours it necessitated had probably played a significant part in his decision not to start a second family. He had entered for this event with his regular training partner who had a reputation for bravado and unthinking recklessness within the circle of their mutual friends. He had collapsed and seriously jeopardised his health on two previous occasions participating in similar events. She was very worried that her husband would be persuaded by this friend to take part even if the weather conditions made such an activity dangerously hazardous.

She spoke frequently about the danger her husband was subjecting himself to, particularly as climate change meant that the event might take place in very high temperatures. However, over time, it seemed that she had made her husband aware of the dangers and they were both carefully monitoring the weather forecasts; his training partner however continued in his determination to take part, no matter what. As I listened to this material and noticed the way it kept coming into her mind in sessions I was aware that it must carry significance, yet I was unable to judge its import. Its transference meaning is not so difficult to understand: she was making it very clear that if her analyst had any sense he would heed all the danger signals she was providing and would not go through with his plans to relocate. She also made it obvious that only someone unthinkingly reckless would go ahead with his plans in the face of such "weather" forecasts. And it was not that I had not heard these forecasts: indeed, I was very anxious that my patient might break down at some point and that it would be very clear to all who carried the responsibility for this.

It is perhaps surprising then that I had to discuss this material with a colleague before the full meaning of it became clear to me. When my colleague said to me "She is really raising the temperature and making you stew in your guilt" I immediately recognised the truth of his observation and felt foolish not to have seen it fully myself. Very quickly though, I became acutely aware of the fact that I did feel enormously guilty and ashamed about what I was doing. I had not sufficiently acknowledged this to myself; in moving away from London I was inevitably breaking a professional tenet that I had hitherto held dear: the psychoanalyst does not abandon patients. As I admitted this to myself I also had to acknowledge that I was being selfish, putting my own wish for my family and me to live outside London above my concern for my patients. However, with time this became less the source of burning shame and mortification and more something I could ruefully acknowledge as a truth about myself: I *was* making a selfish decision and I *was* guilty of relegating my professional responsibility to my patients to second place in my priorities.

It is interesting to reflect on the fact that the colleague with whom I discussed this material did not immediately grasp the full extent of my feelings of guilt and shame; he took an external point of view and did not see my decision to relocate as anything so terrible; it was my own, insufficiently interrogated, judgement that was so draconian. The more savage version of the superego is usually far harsher than any external critic would ordinarily be. Indeed if the criticism comes clearly and explicitly from the outside it can give the blamed party a better opportunity to contemplate the justice of the charges being brought against him. Left to his own superego and without such external reality checks, the "guilty" person is more likely to stew unthinkingly in his guilt without being able to reflect on his situation.

As I thought about the clinical situation I was able to acknowledge to myself that, while I felt guilty and responsible for my actions, they were not a subject for an ethical committee to consider. Psychoanalytically one could say that this thinking freed me from an intolerant and ruthless internal ethical committee and allowed for a more benign one who found me guilty, but who sympathetically took into account the circumstances of my decision. With this greater self-tolerance there came a more benign attitude to what the patient had been doing to me; my countertransference became a source of interest as *a clinical fact*; prior to this, I had been unconsciously threatened by a dreaded sense of incontestable personal failing.

Thus I regained the state of mind Money-Kyrle (1956) described as being necessary for the countertransference to function as a source of analytic information, characterised by what he called sublimated curiosity, benign "parental" concern and tolerance. This meant that I could regard what my patient was putting me through as her prerogative as a patient − it was her right to actualise a transference in which the dynamics of her relationship with her mother, now repeated with her husband, were re-created, and re-enacted, in the consulting room.

A couple of months after I had told the patient about my forthcoming departure, she again described to me that her husband's training partner continued to disregard all the advice he was given about the folly of his actions and the dangers to which he was exposing himself. In response I described to her the situation as I saw it in the consulting room: that for a number of weeks she had been subtly warning me of what would happen if I did not re-consider my decision to finish her analysis in the coming year. She felt I was disregarding all these warnings and I would be the one to blame when it all went wrong. If I was sensible, like her husband, I would not go through with my decision. In response to this interpretation the patient chuckled and was then quiet for a few moments before saying "I can't deny it". She said this very simply; as far as I could tell it was a straightforward confirmation of what she realised to be true. Subsequent material supported this view.

A few weeks before the end of her analysis, that is to say about eight months after learning of my decision to relocate, the patient brought the following dream: *she was travelling by Tube to her session. The tube stopped at the station which was closest to her place of work and is also in reality the Tube stop for a beautiful London park. There was an announcement that the line further on was closed – passengers were told to disembark. She was indignant about this and found the train guard and began to complain to him. She protested that she was missing an important meeting because of this breakdown in service. The guard suggested that she accept the fact of this and that she use the opportunity to take a walk in the park. Indignantly she said that if she could not go to her meeting she would have to go into work instead. The guard repeated that she could use the opportunity to enjoy the fine weather and beautiful surroundings of the park.*

There the dream ended and she told me that she had woken with it in her mind. Lying awake, she had gone on to think about a course she was planning to teach in the following academic year. She had been determined to make it exemplary and to cover all aspects of the subject. She had then found herself deciding not to do this; she realised that the planning and research she had already done were more than sufficient and so she would not use her summer break to continue this work; she would instead plan a holiday. At that point she had begun to cry, and this had woken her husband – he had tried to comfort her until she had explained to him that she was crying not because she was distressed but because she felt very relieved.

Discussion of clinical material

In his paper on countertransference Money-Kyrle (1956) discussed the situation in which the countertransference is too troubling to the analyst and the emotional disturbance is such that it diminishes his ability to think clearly. The example he gave showed how the analyst was able to regain his composure and his cognitive abilities within a couple of sessions. So I might be embarrassed to be reporting how long it actually took me to realise the extent of my guilt, and that I needed the help of my colleague in order to do so. However, my own clinical experience and my observations in supervision of other clinicians suggest that this lengthy period in which the analyst does not understand fully what is going on is not at all unusual. This is so when a fundamental issue is being enacted in an analysis, and the analyst needs to be able to suffer in a state of incomprehension. Interestingly Money-Kyrle also described a situation which may be particularly disabling of the analyst's functioning: if the analyst:

> cannot tolerate a sense of being burdened with the sense of the patient as an irreparable or persecuting figure inside him, he is likely to resort to a defensive kind of re-projection that shuts out the patient and creates another bar to understanding.
>
> (p. 362)

In the case that I have described a kind of dread had disabled me from seeing what became clear when my supervisor described it. It was not the case that I had not previously experienced a particular dread with this patient: as I indicated I had delayed telling her of my decision to leave London longer than with my other patients. Other examples of my feeling very aware of her potential unspoken criticism came to my mind as I thought over what my supervisor had said. At the time I had been qualified for about two years so while I was an inexperienced psychoanalyst I had over ten years of clinical experience. I was at least sufficiently experienced to know that I would have to hold the thought, that is, not convey it in the next session but rather to wait until I was reasonably sure that I had de-cathected it of the moralism that had invaded it. That is to say, I had to decontaminate my view of myself as someone who was doing something unspeakable to her, but also crucially, decontaminate my view of her as someone who was doing something unspeakable to me.

When I had wrestled with this dilemma and had de-toxified my judgement from the strict morality which had invaded it, I was in a position to put a very difficult thought to my patient. In effect I said to her that she controlled her objects by insinuating that they were guilty of having wronged her. It was then striking how straightforwardly she accepted this interpretation and that it did not provoke a moralistic attack on herself. I think that my working through of my own guilt, and my anger at her for what she was putting me through, created a tolerance of guilt which had communicated itself to her in the way I made the interpretation. It is also worth noting that she was later able herself to make the links with her behaviour towards her mother and her husband. She was regretful about having behaved like that but not too damning of herself. This was not a once and for all time achievement, but there was undoubtedly a change in her; she could tolerate knowing herself a little better.

Further evidence of this development in her functioning and its consequences are given in the dream and its sequel. When we came to talk about the dream I put to her that I was the guard who had indicated to her that it was permissible to enjoy life in a fuller way – whether that meant taking a walk instead of working, planning a holiday or choosing to live outside London. It is even possible that having an affair could be understood in this light. As the patient broadened her sense of what was "right" for her objects to do, she modified her attitude to herself and it became more possible for her to allow pleasure in her life.

It might be argued that there is an indication of an earlier trauma which the mother's leaving in her adolescence revived; the eczema in her early childhood and its return when the mother left certainly suggest this. This might suggest that my analysis of the situation disregarded the possibility that what was dreaded in the analysis by both participants was a breakdown in which she would not be able to hold herself together. This might indeed be so, but I would argue that such a breakdown is in its very essence the product of a moralistic and murderous rage that would destroy any sense of arms that could hold and understand the baby. A suicidal destruction of that part of the baby that knows it needs to be held may also play a significant part in such a breakdown and hence "a nameless dread" and "a fear of falling for ever".

General discussion

Fajrajzen (1973, available in English, 2014) wrote of the ubiquity of the compulsion to make moral judgements which he believed derived from the earliest period of life in which the infant distinguishes between what it experiences as good and what it judges to be bad. He also quoted Freud on the similarity of the tasks undertaken by the therapist and the examining magistrate: both "have to uncover the hidden psychical material" (Freud, 1906, p. 108). In the case of Little Hans Freud wrote: "Analysis replaces the process of repression, which is an automatic and excessive one, by a temperate and purposeful control on the part of the highest agencies of the mind. In a word, *analysis replaces repression by condemnation*" (Freud, 1909, p. 145, original italics). Although Freud wrote this before he had formulated the concept of the superego its importance is clearly indicated in this passage. As early as 1909, Freud was aware of the difference between a draconian judgement that enforces repression by a threat of castration and a more "temperate" agency that can judge less harshly and, while condemning, allows for a process of renunciation and enables the latency period, rather than making for neurotic repression.

The provenance of Bion's term "Language of Achievement" is pertinent to this discussion. He introduced the expression in *Attention and Interpretation* (1970, p. 2). He wrote:

> In his sphere the psychoanalyst's attention is arrested by a particular experience to which he would draw the attention of the analysand. To do this he must employ the Language of Achievement. … [T]he session affords me … an opportunity for drawing attention to the actual phenomena to which I think the analysand should attend …. [T]he Language of Achievement, if it is to be employed for elucidating the truth, must be recognized as deriving not only from sensuous experience but also from impulses and dispositions far from those ordinarily associated with scientific discussion.

I take this latter sentence to mean that the truth which the psychoanalyst aspires to discover, will, at times, have to be garnered from experience which is imbued with human emotion and character and hence resistant to becoming known. This resistance will be internal and will concern knowing about both the self and the object: becoming conscious of both or either will be resisted by the superego.

Bion adopted the term "Language of Achievement" from Keats' description of Shakespeare as a "Man of Achievement". Keats (1817) had written to his brother:

several things dove-tailed in my mind, and at once it struck me what quality went to form a Man of Achievement, especially in Literature, and which Shakespeare possessed so enormously – I mean Negative Capability, that is, when a man is capable of being in uncertainties, mysteries, doubts, without any irritable reaching after fact and reason.

(pp. 477–478)

One reason Keats so admired Shakespeare was that Shakespeare broke with the popular 15th and 16th century tradition of the morality play (Mawson, personal communication). Rather than have his characters personify abstract qualities such as virtue or vice implying a conflict between right and wrong from which a moral message might be drawn, Shakespeare allowed his characters a much greater complexity and nuance. It is in this way that he was able to be, and enabled his audience to be, "in uncertainties, mysteries, doubts, without any irritable reaching after fact and reason" and without, one might add, any irritable reaching after a moral position. Shakespeare was thus able to speak what Bion came to call the Language of Achievement in order to describe *what is*, without simultaneously intending to imply *what should be*. We might say that the analytical task is to describe what is happening without a strict moral judgement, always bearing in mind that it is the patient's prerogative to be himself or herself, warts and all, and it is the clinician's responsibility to put into words an understanding of what the patient is doing.

The problem is how to talk to the patient *without writing a morality play*, so to speak, whether it be on the subject of our own inadequacies or the patient's failings. While we seek to speak the Language of Achievement it is very easy to use the same words in order not to communicate a thought but to communicate a damning moral judgement, or, as a reaction formation, to try to communicate a complete absolution of any fault or blame.

I have frequently had the experience in supervision of bringing the supervisee's attention to what I think is happening in the relationship between patient and clinician and for the latter to say with some anxiety "Would you actually say that to the patient?". The implication is that the clinician can see some truth in what I am describing; it resonates with their experience with the patient; but they feel that they would transgress some code if they were to use that experience in formulating an interpretation. Such a moment

64

captures the move from dread to anxiety: what had hitherto been dreaded has now been described in words and the immediate response is one of anxiety. I remember one supervisee agreeing with me about my understanding of the way his patient consistently belittled his analyst's contributions and that he would need to take this up more robustly; he added that this would be the "killer" interpretation. Consciously he intended to communicate the potential effectiveness of such an intervention but he also conveyed the nature of the dread that had kept him previously unaware of this aspect of his counter-transference; he dreaded the murderous rage he felt towards his patient in response to her treatment of him.

In my introduction I quoted Freud on a number of occasions referring to dread but in fact his use of the actual word is somewhat inconsistent – he did try to delineate it exactly but thereafter used it interchangeably with the terms "anxiety" and "fear". (See the foot-note on page 13 of Freud, 1920. There are also the difficulties of translation from German to English which further complicate the exact semantics.) However, Freud did offer a study of "what arouses dread and horror" (p. 219) in his analysis of Hoffmann's story of the Sandman (Freud, 1919). I won't attempt to précis the story other than to say that the Sandman is a figure that completely terrifies the main protagonist of the story, Nathaniel, a terror that finally compels Nathaniel to destroy himself physically by throwing himself off a high tower. Freud argued that what produced the feeling of the uncanny in the story is that the figure of the Sandman is both strange (*unheimlich*) and somehow familiar (*heimlich*). In trying to understand this Freud argued that the Sandman is in effect a repre-sentation of a malignant and murderous father, completely split off from aspects of the good father.

Freud's paper is interesting from a historical perspective since when he wrote it he was clearly conceptualising the main phase of superego development as being "heir to the Oedipus complex" (Freud, 1923, p. 48). He wrote, in the "Uncanny" paper:

> When all is said and done, the quality of uncanniness can only come from the fact of the "double" (the terrifying split off aspect of the self) being a creation dating back to a very early mental stage, long since surmounted – a stage, incidentally, *at which it wore a more friendly aspect.*
>
> (1919, p. 236)

As was discussed in Chapter 2, Klein was to take the concept of the death instinct that Freud was developing at the same time as he wrote "The 'uncanny'" and use it to elaborate a picture of a terrifying early superego which had no such "friendly aspects". However it is also interesting that later in his paper Freud did hint that it was the emotions that arise from the move from the "heimlich" womb to the "unheimlich" external world that produces a dread (p. 245). I conceptualise this as a consequence of the infant's murderous rage at being expelled into the reality of extra-uterine life with its complement of both good and bad experiences; as Fajrajzen (2014) pointed out this immediately brings into contention the ability to distinguish good and bad.

I was once in the position of sitting in the same room as a mother feeding her infant at the breast. The door bell sounded and on answering it I was confronted with a delivery man who insisted that he obtain the signature of the mother before he could leave his parcel. Thus I was left literally holding the baby, only for a minute or so, but I was in no doubt that as well as fury I was also observing moral outrage, a sense that this was absolutely not how the world should be ordered or how a mother should behave. In that minute I observed the infant's destructive rage against the world. My arms and then her mother's arms that tried to hold and comfort her after she had been handed back to her mother, were violently dismissed as totally inadequate to deal with the scale of the catastrophe that had befallen her. It also appeared that she was destroying her own fledgling sense that, while this break in her feeding was unexpected, she had sufficient experience (she was then about fourteen weeks old and had a mother who was devoted to her) to know that normal service would be restored as soon as possible. She was also destroying, it seemed to me, her sense that in such distress she needed to be held and comforted. This seemed indicative of what Bion called an attack on one's own ego functions. Such a conceptualisation and dating of the more extreme and malignant superego would be more in keeping with the view later developed by Klein.

Bion (1962) wrote that the infant's envy of the breast destroyed the possibility of a commensal relationship and left the infant with a sense of nameless dread. In clarifying the consequences of this difficulty between container and contained he underlined the role of the pathological superego. Writing of the object that is encountered and then re-introjected in such a situation he stated: "there is an envious assertion of moral superiority without any morals" (p. 97). This

> shows itself as a superior object asserting superiority by finding fault with everything ... any tendency to search for the truth ... is met by destructive attacks on the tendency and the reassertion of the "moral" superiority. ... The power to arouse guilt is essential ... [this] contrasts ... with conscience in that it does not lend itself to constructive activity.
>
> (p. 98)

While Bion's emphasis in *Learning from Experience* was on the role of the infant's envy in this failure of development, in "Attacks on linking" (1959) he had stressed the object's resistance to acceptance of the infant's projections; in this respect he was perhaps closer to Winnicott in his emphasis on the role of deprivation and environmental failure. To return briefly to my presented case: envy was certainly a factor in the patient's personality, as I briefly indicated, but it was not possible in the analysis to re-construct the history of this problem; what appeared to help was the working through of the problems posed by the assertion of moral superiority in the transference–countertransference matrix. The genesis of a superego that behaves in this way was not clarified, but the struggle of both participants to come to terms with their tendency to behave in this way was evident, and their struggles with this predisposition was eventually transformative to a significant degree.

While it is not possible to argue from one case I would like to consider that my understanding of my dilemma demonstrates what is frequently dreaded by the analyst: that he will come to a thought, based on his experience with the patient, that, spoken directly, will strip the patient of any sense of worth. That is to say what is dreaded is a pathological superego that sees everything and condemns everything. This I think is one meaning of "falling for ever" – there are no arms to reach out and support and to help take a balanced view. While it is the analyst's pathological superego that is central to this clinical picture it also has to be borne in mind that patients differ in their inclination to stimulate this propensity in the analyst. As I argued in the previous chapter: while Strachey (1934) was correct in his view that psychoanalytic progress in the patient corresponds to a lessening of the severity of his/her superego, he underestimated the emotional strain this process puts upon the psychoanalyst. I suggested there that it is the analyst who has to temper his superego before the patient is able to do so. I think Mrs D's case illustrates this process and the countertransferential difficulties that this poses.

My experience suggests that one is never free from the "daemonic power" that can fuel one's sadism. No matter how mature the analyst may feel himself to be, he will never be entirely free of a tendency to regress to earlier states of mind and an inclination to judge on the crude basis of "That is right" or "That is wrong". This will be particularly so when the clinical situation is as fraught with tension as was the case with Mrs D after I had informed her of my departure.

In Chapter 2 I quoted John Steiner remembering his analysis with Hanna Segal and writing:

> I think Hanna Segal's kindness was accompanied by a respect for truth and indeed her kindness made truth more acceptable and less persecuting …. [T]ruth without kindness is not really true, but we would add that kindness without truth is not really kind.
>
> (Steiner, 2013)

I presume that the first part of that statement "Truth without kindness is not really true" refers to the fact that if the clinician endeavours to speak the truth without working through and hence modifying the harshness he might feel, then he is not being true to his conscious intent, which is to help the patient know him- or herself better. I have argued that the analyst needs to be anxious about his capacity to be unkind and that, at times and with certain patients, a dread that he may become harshly and forensically truthful can cloud his clinical thinking.

4

THE PSYCHOANALYST'S EGO IDEALS

Introduction

Bion is credited with the statement that the intention of the psychoanalyst is to introduce the patient to the person he spends all his life with, namely his own self. I have suggested (Sedlak, 2016) that alongside this there has to be a related goal which is to make that self-knowledge *tolerable* to the patient. This in turn implies that a relatively successful psychoanalysis will enable the patient to expand their emotional range and its resilience. This will allow for internal and external realities, which had previously been defended against, to be perceived and experienced along with the emotions that they give rise to. To paraphrase Bion again: the patient is more able to suffer his emotions rather than to suffer from the consequences of avoiding them. From a psychoanalytical point of view, it is healthier to be aware of and suffer one's guilt about some action or thought rather than to deny it and then suffer from some self-damaging act.

The psychoanalytic setting and the analytic process are designed to facilitate this development. The setting is such that the patient's habitual ways of construing and relating to the world are revealed, at least to the trained eye and ear of the psychoanalyst, who hears the patient's free associations as derivatives of the patient's perceptions of the transference relationship and understands them as a means of describing and affecting that situation. The analyst then interprets his understanding to the patient who thus has an opportunity to learn something about himself and, so the theory goes, tolerate this knowledge because of the tolerant, neutral atmosphere in which the knowledge is communicated (Strachey, 1934). As Strachey himself described, things can go wrong in this process, and he detailed the analyst's frequently observed reluctance to give a clear and concise interpretation of what he understands to be happening. I proposed in Chapter 2 that this difficulty might not be, as Strachey suggested, due to the analyst's fear of the patient's aggressive response, but rather because of the analyst's trepidation about revealing his own aggressive and critical stance towards the patient. That is to say the analyst will not have been able, under the pressure of the clinical situation, to maintain or attain a neutral and tolerant stance and will reveal himself to be precisely the sort of critical figure that the patient fears.

When I presented an earlier version of Chapter 2 to a scientific meeting of the British Society Edna O'Shaughnessy asked a question about the analyst's ego ideals. Having researched this concept I realised that it enabled further exploration of the issue I was investigating: the emotional pressures that the analyst has to contend with in the clinical situation.

I will use a somewhat crude division of the analyst's objectives in suggesting that he will aspire to be an investigator, a discoverer of something approximating to a truth about the patient's way of being; I will call this the analyst's psychoanalytic ego ideal. I will suggest that at times this will be in conflict with another ego ideal which I will call a depressive or reparative ego ideal; it could also be called a parental ego ideal in that it aspires to care for and love the patient in the same way that a mother strives to relate to her baby despite the demands he makes upon her. I will examine the antecedents of these ego ideals, the possible conflict between them, and the part that this can play in the process of psychoanalysis with certain patients.

The concept of the ego ideal

Freud (1914c) introduced the concept of the ego ideal in the "Narcissism" paper where he wrote:

> The subject's narcissism makes its appearance displaced on to this new ideal ego, which, like the infantile ego, finds itself possessed of every perfection that is of value. As always where the libido is concerned, man has here again shown himself incapable of giving up a satisfaction he had once enjoyed. He is not willing to forgo the narcissistic perfection of his childhood; and when, as he grows up, he is disturbed by the admonitions of others and by the

awakening of his own critical judgement, so that he can no longer retain that perfection, he seeks to recover it in the new form of an ego ideal. What he projects before him as his ideal is the substitute for the lost narcissism of his childhood in which he was his own ideal.

(p. 94)

In this passage Freud used two different terms: ideal ego and ego ideal. The former refers to an early narcissistic construction in which the infant feels itself to be "possessed of every perfection". Freud took this to be something akin to a platonic conception to which the ego forever aspires, although this takes on more realistic aspects and becomes an ego ideal or ego ideals (in *Group Psychology and the Analysis of the Ego*, Freud made the point that the ego ideal is built on "the most various models", 1921, p. 129). Nevertheless, these constructions will always be driven to some degree by the ego's earliest longing to love itself and be loved by its introjected objects (the superego). As I will demonstrate this longing for narcissistic perfection is ubiquitous even in relatively mature functioning.

When Freud introduced the term ego ideal he had not yet formulated the concept of the superego, but in the "Narcissism" paper he did indicate that they could be thought of as different, although related, concepts. He wrote: "For the ego the formation of an ideal would be the conditioning factor of repression" (Freud, 1914c, p. 94). He was suggesting that once an ideal has been established, any thought, phantasy or emotion which might betray that the ideal is not being lived up to, may be repressed. He implied that this would be due to a fear of a critical agency, which he came later to call the superego. This distinction between an ideal that one aspires to, and a psychical structure which judges one when one does not live up to that ideal is relatively clear:

It would not surprise us if we were to find a special psychical agency which performs the task of seeing that narcissistic satisfaction from the ego ideal is ensured and which, with this end in view, constantly watches the actual ego and measures it by that ideal.

(1914c, p. 95)

This distinction is maintained in the *Introductory Lectures* (1916, 1917b) but in *Group Psychology* (1921) and thereafter in *The Ego*

71

and the Id (1923) the distinction between the ego ideal and the superego began to blur in Freud's writing, and in the latter work the terms are used interchangeably. In 1933 in *New Introductory Lectures on Psycho-Analysis* (1933a) Freud subsumed the ego ideal under a broad definition of the superego so that the latter had the three functions of "self observation, of conscience and of the ideal" (p. 66).

Sandler et al. (1963) considered that some essential distinction was lost when Freud equated the ego ideal with the superego in 1923 and then later subsumed it in the comprehensive definition of the superego. They described how later authors found Freud's original conceptualisation of the ego ideal as a separate structure from the superego to be clinically useful. Reich (1954, 1960) saw the formation of the ego ideal in "primitive" and "archaic" identifications with idealised infantile objects. She suggested that the "ego ideal expresses what one desires to be; the superego, what one ought to be" (1954, p. 218).

Jacobson (1954) also emphasised the sense of unity with the primary object as the early model for the ego ideal and noted its lifelong tenacity:

> This double face of the ego ideal, which is forged from ideal concepts of the self and from idealized features of the love objects, gratifies indeed the infantile longing of which we said that it is never fully relinquished: the desire to be one with the love object ... our never ending struggle for oneness between ego and ego ideal reflects the eternal persistence of this desire.
>
> (p. 107)

The fact that the term ego ideal was used by Freud in different senses at different points will have played a part in its relative relegation as a recognised and utilised concept. I would also suggest that much of the literature that might have focused on the ego ideal has been subsumed under the rubric of the broader term "narcissism", and investigations into various forms of pathological and healthy narcissism also made the term increasingly redundant. In many papers on narcissism an ego ideal is implicitly or sometimes explicitly described. Reich's 1960 paper is a case in point.

Chasseguet-Smirgel (1975, English translation, 1985), is probably the analyst who has made most use of the ego ideal concept. She related the development of a more realistic ego ideal to the Oedipal phase: as the child grows up he is admonished by others for his Oedipal strivings and he becomes aware of the reality of generational differences so that, to some extent at least, he has to modify his ego ideal. Without wishing to deny the importance of the Oedipal situation, I think that at every developmental stage there will be modifications in the form that the ego ideal takes. However, the same basic need will always seek satisfaction: the need to feel that one approximates to a state of perfection, and the genesis of this need is in the earliest period of life. Such a meta-psychology also emphasises the link between narcissism and the ego ideal and it is in this way that various narcissistic states are linked to the superego (Ingham, 2007).

Chasseguet-Smirgel (1985) neatly summarised that the ego ideal is the heir to primary narcissism just as the superego is, in classical theory, the heir to the Oedipus complex. (I will not enter here into the controversy about the status of the primary narcissism concept (Stolorow, 1975), nor into the issue about the accuracy of the translation employed by Chasseguet-Smirgel (Quinodoz, 2010).)

To summarise: the ego ideal is a model of oneself to which one aspires because to be judged to be equal to the ego ideal is to experience a self-regard and a love for the self. The links to narcissism are much clearer than with the superego concept, and the differentiation of the superego in form and function from the ego ideal concept follows. The ego ideal is how one would wish to be; when one fails to achieve such ambitions one is judged by a different but related mental structure: the superego.

The analyst's ego ideals and conflict between them

Naturally the psychoanalyst will have ego ideals and will be judged by his superego, harshly or benignly as the case may be, if he fails to achieve these aims. There is a limited literature on the analyst's ego ideal. Solomon (1992) quoted Grinberg as having written: "The analyst's identity ... is based on integrity, ethics, and love of truth. These attributes are manifestations of the analyst's ego ideal and superego." Clinical reality is such that the analyst will occasionally find that his "integrity, ethics, and love of truth" are compromised by the emotional pressures of the clinical situation. For instance, Feldman (1997) discussed the analyst's versions of himself with which the analyst is comfortable and noted that this can lead to the analyst being at least temporarily insensitive to the broader spectrum of the clinical situation. He described feeling comfortable with a sense of himself (his ego ideal, although he does not use the term) as an "unruffled observer"; this temporarily disabled him from seeing that he was contemporaneously being experienced by his patient as a negligent and uncaring object who saw disturbance and confusion in his patient and denied any responsibility for its cause. This would be an example of an allegiance to discover the truth conceding to a pressure to identify with an ego ideal.

At other times the ideal aim of being able to maintain an objective distance may be sacrificed to the ego ideal of being a good and trustworthy carer. The following vignette is taken from the supervision of an experienced male psychotherapist. A patient came for a consultation insisting from the outset that the therapist must acknowledge as a fact that she had been the victim of an abusive childhood. She indicated that no therapeutic relationship would be viable unless the therapist consented to this view. This was a difficult beginning to the consultation, and the therapist reported that he felt "on trial". Eventually he interpreted that the patient felt that she had had no one in her past who would want to listen to her distress about the abuse and believe it had happened, and she desperately wanted the therapist to do so. This sounded like a reasonable enough interpretation but the therapist reported to me that he had interpreted under duress and as a means of dealing with the pressure the patient was exerting upon him. Implicit in his interpretation was an acknowledgement that the abuse had occurred. The session became flat after this despite the patient's apparent relief following his interpretation and her ready agreement to its veracity. She had gone on to complain about a number of people who "did not take her seriously" but she did this in a monotonous and aggrieved way which did not allow for further exploration and the therapist was left disappointed with the consultation.

He told me that he had not wanted to take up with the patient his experience of the threat and coercion the patient had exerted for fear that she would experience this in itself as abuse and would walk out of the session. Thus he had put to one side his sense of being forced to think in a particular way, and had instead adapted his intervention. This is the kind of interaction in which the clinician feels, as Tuckett observed:

anxiety and worries about being judgemental … [some] patients do not easily take to the provision of a neutral rather than affirmative environment, because they feel that if the analyst is not with them then she/he is against them.

(2011, p. 1387)

So my supervisee's interpretation avoided the analysis of the current emotional reality of the session and he had instead provided the patient with what she had insisted on: the therapist's acquiescence to the fact of her abuse. Further material supported the view that this was an error since she had gone on to complain that people "did not take her seriously"; this may be taken as a confirmation that she felt that the therapist too had failed to appreciate and consider her dilemma. A deeper consideration of the transference–countertransference matrix might have revealed a situation in which coercive force and a threat of dire consequences were being used to ensure compliance. In acting as though he believed the patient could recognise and respond to a safe environment the therapist might really have not taken seriously what the aftermath of abuse was for this patient (Milton, 1994). This is not to say that had he acted differently and interpreted the coercion she was applying upon him, then there would have been a more satis-factory outcome; it is not possible to know. In fact, she did not attend follow-up appointments.

This example illustrates the conflict a clinician often feels between one ego ideal, that of the therapist who is able to provide a safe and trustworthy setting for the patient, and another ego ideal, the professional who is able to explore unconscious functioning without compromise. It was probably such situations that Widlöcher (1978, p. 388) had in mind when he wrote:

More radically the patient attempts to destroy the psychoanalyst's ego ideal, and to take his place by placing the analyst in a state of dependence upon the patient. The psychoanalyst's ego ideal is an unacceptable formation to the patient, for it is seen as a rival. Many negative therapeutic reactions constitute examples of this mechanism … it is as if the patient intended to give notice to the psychotherapist as follows: "You will not succeed with me. Your ideal cure will be blocked" – a form of testing which conceals a demand: "Show me that you love me all the same, and that you love me more than the goal you have set yourself by taking me on

75

and the narcissistic reward which you receive when it is attained."
The patient, like any child, wants to be loved for himself, and not
as a function of the parental narcissistic ideal. The child wants to be
the sole love object. The ego ideal is accurately perceived as a rival
which the patient wishes to destroy.

Widlöcher was writing of the analyst's psychoanalytical ego ideal but
implying that this may clash with another ego ideal of a trustworthy
and safe carer; he was also suggesting that some patients will be sensitive to this. My supervisee's patient may have used this dilemma
to commit an incestuous act herself by forcing her therapist into a
particular relationship with her and away from the relationship he
had with his discipline. Widlöcher's formulation is also of interest
because he indicated the role of the analyst's narcissism in his ego
ideal of being a professional who helps his patients by applying his
analytic craft.

Cooper (1986) in discussing the analytic attitude implied that the
analyst will have to maintain a balance between at least two ego
ideals. One is based on an identification with an ideal parent who
is dedicated to the care of his patient, doesn't give up on them, is
endlessly patient and forever trying to understand. This attitude at its
extreme becomes a therapeutic zeal, which can leave the analyst
prey to the patient's control, as in my example above. It needs to be
balanced by an ability to keep an enquiring distance, that is to say an
ego ideal which is based upon an identification with analytical parents. However, Cooper argued, there too lies a danger: if this latter
identification becomes extreme it can lead to what he termed
"excessive therapeutic nihilism", that is, a pre-occupation with
making the "correct" interpretation without sufficient concern
or enquiry into its effect upon the patient. At its most extreme the
analyst can act as if he intends to "cure the patient even if it kills
him [the patient]" (Grier, personal communication).

In a later paper, Cooper (2008) traced the origins of these conflicted ideals to the earliest days of psychoanalysis. In "Recommendations to physicians practising psycho-analysis" (1912), Freud
cautioned his colleagues against entertaining ambitions to heal the
patient and he advised that psychoanalysts should "model themselves
during psycho-analytic treatment on … a surgeon of earlier times
[who] took as his motto the words: 'Je le pansai, Dieu le guérit' [I
dress the wound, God heals it]". If he does otherwise, the analyst

"will not only put him[self] in a state of mind which is unfavourable for his work, but will make him[self] helpless against certain resistances of the patient" (p. 115). Freud was warning his colleagues against becoming over-involved with patients due to a sense of clinical responsibility since this could obscure the ability to take up psychoanalytically the patient's material. Many psychoanalysts have since written of the analyst's need to forgo the ambition of curing the patient; it is one of the elements underlying Bion's (1970) advice to abandon memory and desire. An excellent exposition of this view was given by Caper (1992) who emphasised that the work of the analyst is to do analysis, which is essentially to "only concern himself with giving an accurate, intelligible description of what the patient is doing in the transference and in his internal world, to whom he is doing it, and why". The analyst in Caper's view should not concern him- or herself with whether this leads to "healthy" development but only to try to understand the kind of development that ensues.

Collins (1980) argued that Freud's disclaimer that he was a "therapeutic enthusiast" (1933a, p. 151) was not totally convincing and was done more in order to distance himself from Ferenczi's "need to cure and to help" of which he wrote rather disparagingly (1933b, p. 229). At that time Freud thought it imperative to establish psychoanalysis as a treatment distinct from cure by suggestion. Cooper (2008) considered that the legacy of this could be seen in the difficult situation that many analysts experienced in the United States in the 1950s:

> The concern at the time was how to reconcile the residual effects of Freud's surgical metaphor for analytic process ... with the actuality of the analytic situation – in which the analyst, as well as the patient, ... consciously or unconsciously, is involved in the full array of emotional responses that will arise in any longstanding, intimate relationship.
>
> (pp. 103–104)

Cooper went on to describe the fear in many analysts that they would be judged to be not proper analysts unless they maintained strict neutrality and avoided any deviation from classical analytic technique. He suggested that it was an attempt to reconcile this conflict that led to Greenson's (1965) argument that the analyst should simultaneously analyse the transference and promote a working alliance, an argument that ultimately failed because of the realisation that the working alliance was an aspect of the transference. (This debate in the States in the 1950s and 1960s is also discussed in Chapter 7.)

There is now a far greater tolerance of analytic plurality; counter-transferential enactment is now seen as inevitable and potentially informative; what were once described as "parameters" i.e. changes in the analyst's internal setting which were considered to be mistakes or failures to maintain an analytic stance and setting (Eissler, 1953) are frequently described as advances in proper analytic technique. However, at times there continues to be a necessary conflict between what I will call a reparative ego ideal and a psychoanalytical ego ideal which aims to act in accordance with acknowledged psychoanalytical theory and technique and with the clear objective of arriving at a view of the patient which approximates to a truth. Efforts to reconcile these differing ideals, such as those of Greenson (1965) and Poland (2002) are helpful, but I consider that these tensions are inevitable in everyday practice, and the clinician's unavoidable task is to struggle with them in an attempt to contain them.

The psychoanalyst's depressive/reparative ego ideal

It is doubtful if a real forgoing of a wish or a need to help the patient is achievable or even advisable. I would concur with Pontalis who describes the psychoanalyst's wish to cure as an "uncurable idea" (quoted in Baranger et al., 1983, p. 10). The wish to be reparative must be one of the primary conscious and unconscious reasons for choosing to be a psychoanalyst. Being a professional working in the field of mental health carries a responsibility to seek to help the patient and to audit, however informally, one's ability to do so.

Bader (1994) argued that what he calls "only to analyze" may become an attitude that encompasses a dereliction of professional duty. He quoted Leo Stone:

I cannot give serious recognition to any conception of psycho-analytic practice in which these [therapeutic] purposes are not the primary and central consideration of the analyst. ... Our knowledge and our methods were born in therapy. I know of no adequate rational motivation for turning to analysis – and persisting in it through its deeper vicissitudes – other than the hope for relief of personal suffering.

(p. 425)

In the same vein, Greenson (1965) wrote:

> In my personal experience, I have never known an effective psychoanalytic therapist who did not feel strongly a desire to relieve the suffering of his patients. I have met M.D. psychoanalysts who were essentially misplaced researchers or data-collectors, and their therapeutic results were below expectations.
>
> (p. 404)

A number of analysts have written of the wish to help being an indispensable part of the character structure of the analyst. Langer (1962) considered that:

> for an analyst to be a therapist or a real investigator or both, something ... is needed: something that we might define as a passion for his profession. And this passion, which differentiates him from the opportunist, derives not only from his "capacity for communication" or from his "wish to help", but from his need to do so, a need characteristic of any real vocation.

She argued that this need to make reparation is:

> the feeling of being summoned by an internal voice (the superego) to the realization of a determination. The authentic analyst, like the authentic physician, feels called upon to repair parts of his ego (his infantile ego) and his damaged internal objects.
>
> (p. 274)

To re-state this in terms of the ego ideal: in order to love himself, and to gain satisfaction from the work, the analyst needs to feel that he is a healer, making reparation.

Ella Sharpe (1950) addressed some of these issues and the dangers that stem from an inadequate grasp of one's motivation when she wrote:

> [our personal] [a]nalysis should have given us the knowledge of why we have become psycho-analysts. We should know the

unconscious roots of a major sublimation of this kind ... know the deep-seated gratification that we get from the work, in order that deep-lying anxieties may be recognized and resolved in their true connections and not superficially explained. The physician will not shirk the analysis of those deep-lying anxieties from which his medical skill gets its drive. The drive to heal the body is inseparable from the anxiety-ridden sadism of the primitive levels of the mind that ... desires to hurt and kill. He will recognize that his anxieties about that deep-seated sadism are annulled all the time by healing and curing. In the wish to heal and cure he annuls his own fears before ever the patient as such is considered. Technique will always be vitiated if the physician has not come to grips with the fact that his work itself is a nullification of his own anxieties. The urge, in view of these, will be to cure, and cure does not come that way at all in psycho-analysis. Cure comes by ability to analyse, and hidden anxiety to get a cure may cause havoc to technique, for technique has to be suited to the tempo and peculiarities of the individual, not driven by our own inner necessity to make a patient well. ... If one feels re-assured and pleased at every expression of benefit by the patient, at every disappearance of symptoms, if one feels discouraged at every recrudescence of symptom and misery, one is not immune from one's own anxiety. It means that our own anxiety is annulled by curing, and it is intensified if we do not get assurance. Now the patient's cure does not come about through nullification of our anxiety, not even through our desire to cure him, but only by our ability to analyse resistances to the unconscious. I believe that our infantile sadism and consequent anxiety in the deepest levels makes it always imperative for us to seek an assurance of security. The more that deep level is brought to consciousness and analysed in ourselves, the more we can seek for real and not phantastic assurances – the more we can tolerate the affects of other people, externally in our reality contacts and analytically with patients.

(pp. 258–259)

It is noteworthy that Sharpe does not argue that the analyst will reach a stage of development in which he stops seeking the assurance that the patient's improvement gives him; she argues instead for the analyst's awareness of this unavoidable tendency. The more this is "brought to consciousness" the more able the analyst may be to resist an insistence on improvement in the patient (a cure by suggestion) and correspondingly, more able to resist a scotomisation of resistance in the patient.

The wish to be loved and to love oneself takes a particular form in the depressive phase of development and then develops further, for instance into the ego ideal of a parent. And in some people it finds its later expression in the choice of a career. Loewald (1960) described the similarity between the two roles thus:

> The parent–child relationship can serve as a model here. The parent ideally is in an empathic relationship of understanding the child's particular stage of development, yet ahead in his vision of the child's future and mediating his vision to the child in his dealings with him. This vision, informed by the parent's own experience and knowledge of growth and future, is, ideally, a more articulate and more integrated version of the core of being that the child presents to the parent .... In analysis, if it is to be a process leading to structural changes, interactions of a comparable nature have to take place.
>
> (p. 229)

To my mind, having a vision of a patient's future, while perhaps at times unavoidable and akin to wishing the patient well, can become a slippery slope unless it is contained by a relationship with another ego ideal.

The development of the professional/psychoanalytical ego ideal

Clearly the wish to be reparative from personal motives will not suffice; a professional training is also required. The process of acquiring a professional identity is complex.

While the analyst's professional ego ideal will be a composite structure a particular facet will derive from an identification with admired colleagues, particularly in the early stages of one's career. Britton (2003, pp. x–xi) pointed out that it takes a very long time to gain an amount of experience as a psychoanalytic clinician that is substantial enough to allow one to exercise one's craft in a way that is relatively independent of received

81

wisdom. To appropriate and imitate the qualities of admired or idealised objects is part of the normal development of the psychoanalytic clinician. It is only with time and emotional development that some progress is made from what might be called identifications with ego ideals.

In one of his Italian seminars, Bion (2005, p. 13) said:

> what you have to do is to give the germ of a thought a chance. You are sure to object to it; you are sure you wish it conformed to some cherished psychoanalytic theory, so that if you said it to some other psychoanalyst it could be seen to be in accordance with psychoanalytic theory, or the theories of your supervisor or your analyst ... you have to *dare* to think and feel whatever it is that you think or feel, no matter what your society or your Society thinks about it, or even what *you* think about it.

While apparently advocating the analyst's emancipation from ego ideals, Bion in effect offered the psychoanalyst an attractive and appealing ego ideal: the psychoanalyst courageously able to think independently, immune from pressures whether they be from the patient or from his internal objects or from his colleagues. This is akin to the ego ideal recommended by Freud of the surgeon as a model of an appropriate emotional distance. It is also reminiscent of the similarity Freud observed between the task of the psychoanalyst and the examining magistrate that I noted in the previous chapter: both "have to uncover the hidden psychical material" (Freud, 1906 p. 108). In the case of Little Hans Freud wrote: "Analysis replaces the process of repression, which is an automatic and excessive one, by a temperate and purposeful control on the part of the highest agencies of the mind. In a word, *analysis replaces repression by condemnation*" (Freud, 1909, p. 145, original italics).

As I mentioned in the previous chapter, Fajrajzen (1973, available in English, 2014) examined the way that this identification with Freud as a forensic investigator can easily transform and give expression to the ubiquitous compulsion to make moral judgements. Greenson (1965) probably had something similar in mind when he argued that an excessive abstinence from empathic identification with the patient could lead to analysts taking an "austere, aloof, and even authoritarian attitude toward their patients" (p. 99).

One process involved in freeing oneself from a slavish aspiring to be like one's professional ego ideal(s) is that of mourning as I described in a previous paper (Sedlak, 2016):

> Progress from this state of mind shares many of the features of the working through of earlier identifications (whether with Oedipal parents or the breast); it is a process of painful renunciation and the work of mourning. In Mourning and Melancholia Freud (1917a) described the painful course of mourning, separating valued qualities of the object from oneself, realising that they belong to the other and mourning the fact that one does not have possession of them. Precisely by these means representations of these qualities become established in the ego. Hanna Segal (1991, p. 40) made the same point in a different way when she wrote that only what has been mourned can be symbolised, the point being that when something has been mourned its representation is established in the mind. The paradox is that if one can let something go the outcome is that one internalises it, not by a process of appropriation but by … renunciation.
>
> (p. 1516)

I think when the ego ideal is built up of appropriated professional identifications i.e. when they have been taken in by what might be called acquisitive introjection, it will be an ego ideal that has higher and more exacting standards. Hence the perceived discrepancy between the actual ego and the ideal ego will be such that it will excite the attention of the more pathological version of the superego.

Alongside a process of mourning a related development also takes place. When Freud wrote of the ego's selection of an external figure as an ego ideal: "what he projects before him as his ideal is the substitute for the lost narcissism of his childhood in which he was his own ideal", he indicated that external objects are perceived as having the omnipotence of early narcissism. This insight is salutary: one's external objects, with which one identifies, may not in fact have the qualities that one projects onto them. That is to say, a process of disappointment with one's object is also necessary and this too involves mourning; the perfection that one's professional ego ideal seemed to represent is realised to be in part a narcissistic creation.

Bion's advice to be free of pressures coming from others is probably unachievable. The vast majority of psychoanalysts *do* need to feel that their inner objects, including their colleagues, their Society, approve of and support them. Like everyone else psychoanalysts are involved in the management of the discrepancy between their ego ideal and their reality and the suffering imposed by their superego's attention to this discrepancy. This is the very stuff of being human and hence how the analyst deals with this may play an important part in the treatment of some patients.

The analyst's ego ideals and the patient

In my previous clinical example, I demonstrated how the clinician may be inhibited by a fear that he may damage his patient if he is dictated to by the standards set by his psychoanalytic ego ideal. My account also illustrated the patient's sensitivity to the therapist's relationship with his ego ideal: she was able to control him by threatening a situation in which he would feel he had not lived up to his ego ideal as a helpful and trustworthy person. I will now revisit a case which I discussed in a previous paper (Sedlak, 2003) in which the patient's perception of how the clinician related to his ego ideals allowed for some clinical development.

Mr C was an academic in his thirties when he came for treatment because of his difficulties in establishing and maintaining a relationship that might lead to the happy married life that he consciously desired. Typically he became infatuated with a woman and would have idealised fantasies about the life they would lead but, when the ordinary difficulties of a relationship became apparent, he would lose interest and withdraw. He had been doing this since his late teens and as he approached his mid-thirties he had become sufficiently concerned about this to seek treatment. He lived a considerable distance from my practice and hence we met three times a week, from Tuesday to Thursday. The material I am first going to present comes from a Wednesday session in the second year of his treatment.

He began the session in a dispirited mood and said that he was losing interest in his treatment, he had to travel so far for his sessions, was it worth it, should he perhaps think of stopping? This mood surprised me a little since it had been reasonably clear in the past few months that he valued his treatment and was finding it helpful. He had spoken of this only the previous day and about the good weekend he had spent. A little later in the session the patient compared himself unfavourably with the patient he had seen leaving my consulting room as he had waited for his session in his car. She had looked so happy and contented and appeared to be someone who really got on with her life, unlike himself.

This immediately opened up a number of thoughts in my mind centring on his relationship with his younger sister of whom he has been jealous throughout his life and about whom he had been speaking recently. She had just announced that she was pregnant, and he had recounted how pleased their parents had been about this. This was hurtful to him since he had always imagined that their first grandchild would be his son or daughter. All this came to my mind because the patient he had seen leaving the consulting room was heavily pregnant. As the session progressed it was possible to make a number of interpretations, for example, to link his disappointment about the treatment with his anxiety that I would be disappointed in him when I compared him with my other patient. He made various responses that seemed to confirm my understanding, and I thought he was genuinely able to see what had led to his sudden disillusionment with his treatment and to the historical antecedents of this. Throughout the session, even at the beginning when he had been expressing his disappointment with his treatment, I had felt relatively comfortable and was able to maintain an interested and emotionally equable state of mind.

The next day he began by telling me that he had met a psychologist friend the previous evening who had spoken of his doctoral research. It involved investigating the ways that early family life can influence later relationships. My patient had been very taken with this research and thought it was tremendously valuable. As I listened to this I initially thought that the patient was unconsciously referring to my work the previous day and I prepared to say as much when the opportunity presented itself. However, he continued to talk about the psychologist, his good character and many qualifications, and my feelings about this changed and I began to find myself wishing he would move on to other material. I also felt some disappointment and anger that he was apparently dismissing the work we had done the previous day.

A little later in the session the patient told me that later that day he had to go to a faculty meeting at his place of employment. He was looking forward to this because he had tabled an agenda item that a collegial rival of his would have to deal with. He thought that his colleague would find it difficult to answer adequately the various points that would arise and he looked forward to seeing his discomfort as it became clearer that there was an issue that he had not investigated sufficiently well. Eventually I interpreted that he had placed an item on my agenda, namely the problem of having rivalrous feelings. I described how he had put me in a position in which I was to feel rivalrous with the psychologist and I added that he was enjoying seeing me struggle with this difficult situation.

He responded to this with some surprise and said that he did not think that a psychoanalyst would feel rivalrous with an academic psychologist. He said this in a way that implied that a psychoanalyst would naturally consider himself superior to a psychologist. He then remembered that as a student he had gone to hear an eminent psychoanalyst speak and, while the lecture had been extremely impressive, the speaker had made the audience feel that they would never be able to understand things in the way that he could. I interpreted that he believed that I had avoided the painful work of having to deal with feelings such as rivalry and inferiority by becoming a psychoanalyst. Having achieved this superior position I could now make other people feel inferior. The patient found this interpretation amusing and the atmosphere in the session became much warmer. He confirmed that this was indeed his belief about psychoanalysts in general, and me in particular, although he had not been conscious of it before.

This session demonstrates a temporary blind spot in the analyst since it would have been apparent to an observer that the issue of competitiveness, which was so prominent in the Wednesday session, was actualised in the following session, but this time with the analyst feeling the discomforting rivalry. The scotomisation was caused precisely by the analyst's ego ideal not being able to accommodate a sense of being rivalrous with an academic psychologist. The analyst was discomforted by the realisation that he was rivalrous and that he did indeed harbour the opinion that a psychoanalyst's grasp of human nature was superior to that of an academic psychologist. This was further complicated by the fact that the eminent psychoanalyst the patient referred to had been the subject of a widely publicised scandal, a fact that the patient was most probably aware of. He was probably not aware that his analyst had been an academic psychologist who had decided he could better himself by eventually becoming a psychoanalyst. One can see how unerringly the patient had placed an item on his analyst's agenda.

The patient's helpful material about putting an item on his colleague's agenda oriented me to a consideration of my countertransference and is an example of what Cooper (2008) had in mind when he wrote: "the analyst, as well as the patient, whether wittingly or unwittingly, consciously or unconsciously, is involved in the full array of emotional responses that will arise in any long-standing, intimate relationship" (pp. 103–104). An understanding of the inevitable attempt to attain an ego ideal eventually proved useful in that the patient was helped to realise that he had always sought a partner who would make every other man envious. Whenever a woman revealed herself to be less than perfect this possibility was threatened and then he would end the relationship. He continued in therapy for about five years in total and married in the fourth year of the treatment. He told me that his wife was attractive but she was not the exquisitely beautiful high flyer he had always fantasised about. His ego ideal, in essence the narcissistic phantasy of being in a perfect union in which all needs were satisfied, was modified in his treatment. He was helped to contain a little better the unrealistic expectations his ego ideal demanded.

Concluding comment

I have wanted to demonstrate the ubiquity of the ego ideal and the way that the wish to attain a sense of oneself as possessed of perfection and in a union with perfect objects is never abandoned fully. The danger stemming from an ego ideal to the analyst's ability to analyse is well put by Widlöcher:

> the more the psychoanalyst's ego is dependent on his own ego ideal, the more dependent he is on his patient, and conversely, the more dependent on his patient he feels, the more he accentuates his dependence in relation to his ego ideal and reinforces his own superego demands in order to detach himself from this dependence – a genuine vicious circle which introduces the problems of narcissism into the field of countertransference.
>
> (1978, p. 388)

Towards the end of his paper Widlöcher argued that the analyst has the professional duty to try to divest himself of the narcissistic pull of the ego ideal and instead cathect an ability to appreciate reality, including, I would add, the reality of his countertransference. It might be argued that this ability might make for a capacity for humility which would allow the analyst to transcend the narcissistic pull of the ego ideal and to allow for a tolerance of suffering emotions. Hopefully this is achievable to some degree, but as Freud (1914c, p. 94) pointed out "where the libido is concerned, man has here again shown himself incapable of giving up a satisfaction he had once enjoyed". There is no escape from one's narcissism; the seeking of a narcissistic satisfaction from approximating to an ego ideal is ubiquitous and sometimes artfully arranged. One can even become rather proud and celebratory of one's humility.

5

CONTEMPLATING ANALYTIC FAILURE

Introduction

In 1937 in his last substantial contribution to the clinical literature Freud wrote: "Instead of an enquiry into how a cure by analysis comes about (a matter which I think has been sufficiently elucidated) the question should be asked of what are the obstacles that stand in the way of such a cure" (Freud, 1937, p. 221). It is not that he had been unable to consider the limitations of psychoanalysis previously, in the period of his greatest creativity. In 1917 he had written that:

> there are cases in which even the physician must admit that for a conflict to end in neurosis is the most harmless and socially tolerable solution .... It is not his business to restrict himself in every situation in life to being a fanatic in favour of health. He knows that there is not only neurotic misery in the world but real, irremovable suffering as well, ... whenever a neurotic is faced by a conflict he takes flight into illness, yet we must allow that in some cases that flight is fully justified, and a physician who has recognized how the situation lies will silently and solicitously withdraw.
>
> (Freud, 1917b, p. 382)

In the previous chapter I argued that as part of a development as a clinician in which therapeutic zeal is tempered by experience, thus modifying the analyst's ego ideal, the analyst must contemplate the limitations of his approach. If this can lead to a process of mourning of the ideal object of psychoanalysis the analyst is more able to approach his work realistically and be a little freer from the strictures of a professional superego that demands clinical improvement.

Psychoanalysis is a specific form of treatment and it is not helpful in all cases. In my view it is important that the psychoanalyst is able to accept the limitations of his or her therapeutic efforts. The analyst needs to have a sufficiently worked through ambivalence to psychoanalysis and to his or her own analytic capability which acknowledges the limits of the method and the practitioner. Failure to do so can lead the analyst to attempt to modify technique in ways which risk losing some of the essence of the method. Such modifications of technique might lead to short term gain but might also short-circuit an investigation which may ultimately lead to greater and deeper understanding and hence a more radical alteration in the personality. Freud acknowledged the limitations of psychoanalysis when he wrote "the power of the instruments with which analysis operates is not unlimited but restricted". He went on to state in this quotation, as he did on a number of occasions in the last decade of his life, that "the final upshot always depends on the relative strength of the psychical agencies which are struggling with each other" (1937, p. 230). The forces which Freud had in mind were the instincts which the ego was always trying to "control" and to utilise in its struggle for mastery but which could overwhelm the ego. In considering this struggle for mastery Freud is realistic:

> we reach the conclusion that the final outcome of the struggle we have engaged in depends on the *quantative* factors – on the quota of energy we are able to mobilize in the patient to our advantage as compared with the sum of the powers working against us.
>
> (1938, pp. 181–182; Freud's emphasis)

The above quotation is taken from a paper in which Freud considered the limitations of psychoanalytic effectiveness from a metapsychological viewpoint. In papers which are closer to clinical experience it is rare to read of instincts since they are only discerned in their derivative form. However this does not mean that the essence of Freud's discoveries is obsolete but rather that it is more usually stated within a more "experience-near" conceptualisation. In Britain unconscious phantasy and internal object relationships are used as means of modelling or describing the same forces that Freud discovered in his clinical practice and speculated upon in his meta-psychological theorising. Rather than listening out for indications of instinctual life the modern day analyst is more likely to consider the qualities and actions of the people a patient mentions and use these as an indication of the derivatives of instinctual forces. In effect all material is considered for clues to how the patient is orientated to psychoanalytical work.

For example, a patient who had been helped by her therapist to think about the fact that at the age of forty she was running out of time to have children, a fact she had hitherto ignored or treated as insignificant, began a session by saying that in the morning when the alarm went off she kept pushing the snooze button and turning over to go back to sleep. This could be taken as an unconscious communication about her current reluctance to attend to the painful fact that the therapist had drawn her attention to. The practitioner might consider that this is a derivative of the death instinct, in the way that Segal (1993) described her use of the concept, but need not do so in order to grasp adequately the patient's present state. Although there might not be the same emphasis on instinct in daily clinical work as Freud expressed in his meta-psychological theorising, there still exists what he termed the quantitative factor; it is just that now it is conceptualised more in terms of the hold that certain internal objects can have on a patient's mind.

It is the case that in the seventy-five years since Freud's paper there have been significant advances in technique and a greater understanding of the ways that anti-therapeutic factors in the patient can be formulated and interpreted. An example of this would be Rosenfeld's (1971) contribution on pathological narcissism and how this can be understood in terms of internal object relations. Steiner's (1993) work on pathological organisations and psychic retreats demonstrated how such defences and offences can become deeply established and characterological; Rosenfeld's (1971) description of a Mafia-like gang exerting a hold on a patient's mind, pulling him or her away from a creative and dependent relationship, would be an example of such a phenomenon.

The limitations of psychoanalytic efficacy extend to the psychoanalyst as well as to the patient. The fact that the analyst has undergone a personal analysis is no guarantee that he will be able to consider thoughtfully the emotional pressures that he will be subjected to. Freud was realistic about the power of the forces which were ranged against the psychoanalyst's and patient's attempts to undo the neurotic solutions that the patient had arrived at and instituted in his or her personality. He wrote that the patient:

> must find the courage to direct his attention to the phenomena of his illness. His illness itself must no longer seem to him contemptible, but must become an enemy worthy of his mettle, a piece of his personality, which has solid ground for its existence.
>
> (1914a, p. 152)

The implication of this is that the analyst too needs to be prepared for a confrontation with powerful forces "worthy of his [the analyst's] mettle". Our greater understanding of the complexities of the psychoanalytical situation, the effect of emotional forces on the analyst, the need to contain these and the constant danger of some enactment, means that the analyst should approach clinical work with some trepidation, in the knowledge that it will test his or her capacities. Not only will the analyst confront forces which are indeed a part of the patient's personality and hence are overdetermined and well established, but the mettle of his or her own personality, and the ability to subject this to analytic containment, will be tested. Most pertinently the analyst's internal objects and the way that they will support, or not, his struggle not to evade painful reality will be put to the test in an analysis.

A particular capacity of the psychoanalyst which will be of great importance in some cases is precisely the ability to entertain realistic doubt about all three major components of the psychoanalytic situation, namely the patient, the analyst and the method. I will first briefly describe a case from supervision in which a failure to allow for such doubt limited the therapist's ability to understand fully the clinical picture that confronted her. I will then present two cases of my own which can be designated as analytical failures. The first one demonstrates a failure to modify a terrifying superego and the second a failure to accept the strictures imposed by reality.

Dr A

Dr A, an experienced and respected psychotherapist brought a case for supervision of a young woman in her early twenties who she had been seeing for two years at a frequency of three times a week. The patient had had a breakdown after attempting to attend university – she had only lasted a week before returning home. The therapist described the patient as very immature and emotionally undeveloped for a young woman of her age. For instance she had various plans of what she might do with her life which seemed quite unrealistic; when she attempted to put them into action she quickly failed but she did not seem to learn from this, she would instead move on to her next plan.

The therapist told me that the patient would often ruminate on an incident that had occurred when she was thirteen: she had been found cheating in an exam and had been excluded from her school for a few weeks. The therapist described a few sessions to me and this could be done quickly since the patient, after saying "I'm ready" at the beginning of the session, to which the therapist replied "Let's start", would be silent for very long periods; there was actually very little material to report. In the first of our two consultations I suggested to the therapist that the patient was cheating in that she hoped to pass the examinations of moving from childhood to adolescence to adulthood by enacting one of her plans, rather than working through the maturational tasks imposed by the realities of developing a sexual body and leaving home, for example. I suggested that she would use the therapy, not to work, for example on issues of separation (she continued to live unhappily with her parents), but instead would treat the therapy as a plan which would magically result in her being able to lead a satisfying life. I thought this was a form of hoping to get away with cheating, and the therapist found this a useful way of thinking.

She came for a second consultation and described the various ways she had tried to interpret to the patient based on our discussion in the first consultation. However, the patient's behaviour seemed to me to be the same, and all three sessions were able to be presented very quickly since they consisted largely of silence. All three began in the same way: the patient saying "I'm ready" and the therapist replying "Let's start". As I listened to this I was suddenly struck with the thought that something disastrous might have happened during the development of this patient's mind and that she might be one of those patients who cannot, at least for the time being, make any use of psychoanalytical help. I was also very concerned by a couple of oblique references to suicide and I was bothered by the ritualised start to each of the sessions. This allowed me to formulate a more sophisticated view of what was going on between the patient and the therapist – the patient had little, if any, faith in her own capacity to deal with difficulties in a realistic way *and* she believed that her object was similarly incapacitated. That is to say that her object would not be able to consider realistically the possibility that the patient may not be able to use the therapy; in that respect, she was certainly not "ready" and the therapist's immediate reflex of saying "Let's start" denied a space into which might come the thought, "she is not ready and I don't know whether she ever will be".

Of course this is not to say that the patient could not be helped but rather that help would only be possible if the current emotional reality in the therapy could be faced: the patient had little capacity to broach reality *and she believed that the same must be true of her objects.* I give this as an example of the clinical need to be able to doubt whether, in any particular case, a psychoanalytic treatment is indicated and whether it can be of use to the patient.

It is apposite here to mention the issue of assessment for psychoanalysis. When I was at the Tavistock Clinic I learned from David Malan the importance of assessing the patient's ability to sustain commitment and to tolerate frustration, mainly from a consideration of the patient's history of relationships and their work record. Of course this was not sufficient in itself, the quality of the relationship had to be taken into consideration, but the general point I found was of some use. Malan also stressed the patient's response to trial interpretation as a measure of psychological mindedness and I have incorporated this too in my assessment procedures. While Malan was primarily interested in patients' suitability for brief psychotherapy I think his principles apply to assessment for psychoanalytic treatment. However I have not found these measures to be as predictive as one would wish and I tend to abide by Winnicott's reported dictum that goes more or less: "The best assessment for an analysis is an analysis." Thus I have found that patients who fail to meet these broad requirements can have successful treatments. For instance, the first patient described in Chapter 8 aggressively repudiated my trial interpretation that he knew he very much needed an analysis and yet he went on to have a fruitful analysis. Other patients meet the broad criteria, and yet ultimately their analyses are a disappointment, as I shall show in my first example.

Both the patients that I have briefly mentioned already in this chapter illustrate the propensity to disregard very troubling facts and to continue in ignorance of their predicament. I will now describe in more detail my work with a patient who illustrated further this basic difficulty in allowing that painful realities do really exist and have to be negotiated.

Mrs F

Mrs F was a woman in her late thirties who came to see me at a point in her life when she felt unable to cope with the various problems that had been building for a number of years. She was a senior manager in a government agency and over the last few years she had lost her motivation for her work, lost her belief in the aims and values of the organisation she worked for and wanted to leave her job without having any idea of what she might move on to. Her personal life was in a similar state. She had bought a house with her husband, but the realisation had dawned on both of them that they were not really compatible, and so they had separated with the husband moving out of the house. In fact I was to discover that they had suspected that theirs was not a satisfactory relationship even before they had married. At that time however they had come to a mutual decision that their difficulty was a consequence of a lack of commitment on each of their parts. Thus they decided that the solution to their difficulty was not to separate but rather to buy a house together and to marry! Eventually however the truth that they did not particularly get on and had little interest in each other had asserted itself, and they had decided to go their separate ways. Now there was a problem about selling the house, they could not agree on a realistic price that would enable one of them to buy out the other.

Mrs F gave me this information in the initial consultation but there was something about the way that she described it that made it very difficult for me to follow. I realised after a while that the reason for this was that she presented the whole story as one of indecision between two people who otherwise got on well together, rather than the much more bitter and acrimonious dispute that reading between the lines seemed to reveal. This was an early indication of a way she has of smoothing over real problems in the hope that they might eventually go away.

In the consultation I asked her for a dream. She reported two: in the first she was looking at a young member of her staff who was asking her about a "slight" problem that she had with her back. When she turned round to allow the patient to examine the

95

problem the patient could see that her back was terribly disfigured by what appeared to be small monkeys growing out of it and she had the thought that nothing would be able to be done for this young woman. In the second dream she was in her home, which she told me was slowly falling apart in reality as she and her ex-partner each refused to invest in repairs until outright ownership was established. In the dream she was upstairs and noticed that a piece of wallpaper on a sloping ceiling appeared to be damp. She reached up and found that it peeled off and that there was nothing behind it, such as plaster or a wooden roof structure, and that she was gazing at the night sky.

I took these dreams to be communications of her anxieties about coming to the session and getting herself looked at. For instance I said I thought she was very fearful about what I might see and help her to see if we looked at all the problems that she had tried to put behind her. She appeared to go along with this suggestion and expanded on it to say that having a monkey on your back was a means of saying that there was a problem you could not get away from; thus she agreed with me, but she did not go on to consider the possibility of being unable to be helped, as she had dreamed about her young colleague. She seemed to deal with my interpretation by becoming sensible about it and describing how she dealt with problems at work. She gathered her team about her, they fully discussed the problems, they shared views and they slowly moved towards possible solutions. They discussed ways of testing out the solutions and proceeded in a steady way, testing various hypotheses as they went. She told me this in a way that was at first rather impressive, but I then realised that in doing so she had radically lowered the extent of her anxiety. We were now, as it were, two colleagues discussing how to deal with a work problem and there was an undisputed assumption that we would be successful.

This led me to interpret the second dream. I first spoke to her about her fear about herself, essentially that she had dealt with problems by papering over the cracks (a common metaphor which means covering over and denying that problems exist) and was terrified what might be revealed underneath. I said that I thought the way she had dealt with my observation that she feared there was something that was untreatable was an instance of the way that she did this. That is, she apparently took my interpretation seriously but actually she had a means of taking the substance out of it and hence avoiding profound anxiety about herself. I said I thought that she was very concerned that there was no substantial structure that she would be able to employ to deal with her worries.

She responded to this by describing the relationship between her parents. They had been married for many years and as far as she could remember they had never had an argument. They were a very quiet couple who had no friends and few dealings with their few relatives. She had been an only child and had attended a school away from her neighbourhood so that she had had few friends herself. The family had formed a small self-supporting unit that did not seem to have experienced difficulties or conflict. She remembered that the family would watch the television news together and that her mother would frequently comment about all the misery in the world and say that they were the luckiest family on earth since they did not have any difficulties or hardships. The patient then spoke about having recently visited her parents and having told her father how difficult she was finding it at work. He had said that he had once had problems in his job but it had worked out all right in the end; she told me this by way of illustrating how supportive he had been. I must say that I wasn't very impressed with this support but I interpreted this in the transference: I said I thought that she expected me to say that she should come and see me for analysis and that if she did so then every-thing would work out all right in the end. I linked this with what I thought was an underlying anxiety, namely that I had no substance to me; if she took a good look at me she would find there was no solid structure behind my way of working. I later came to think that her second dream might also be a portrayal of her early experience; where a baby might expect to look up and see a substantial mindful mother she had found that she was looking into an empty space.

Thus, in the consultation I focused on two related anxieties: the first was that she was not able to deal with her problems in a realistic substantial way; the second, that she had come to see someone who also had no fundamental means of thinking about difficulties. She was worried about her internal objects and her external objects.

When treatment began, at a frequency of three and then four sessions a week, I had many occasions to interpret a particular mood that she created. I came to call this the "it will be all right in the end" mood. She held to this belief in relation to the difficult long drawn-out situation with her husband, her work problems and most particularly her analysis. She seemed to believe that as

97

long as she attended and spent sufficient time in the same room as me we would arrive at a resolution of her problems.

At times, particularly early on in the analysis, there was something very seductive about the way she created the impression that coming to her sessions was already a great help to her and that of course it would help her even more substantially in the future. She seemed genuinely grateful for my efforts to help her and she showed a confidence in me and the analysis so that it was very tempting to subscribe to the belief that it would all be all right in the end. Furthermore, it was also the case that to challenge this belief, or even to point out that there was little actual evidence to support it, felt like a very spoiling thing to do. It meant that rather than being experienced as helpful she felt me to be threatening her balance and her stability.

I came to think that my patient was trying to create a seemingly good relationship behind which there lurked a terrible one: that is, behind the soothing facade of it all being all right, there was a patient who did not believe she could be helped since there was no one who would have the substantial resources to help her. Thus I would feel that if I interpreted without challenging her I was colluding in a lie; if I spoke in terms of what I thought was actually happening then I was taking away from her means of managing, and thus exposing her to a calamitous depression. I came to think that this was an experience she had had in her childhood: she had felt that she could either go along with her parents' view that everything in their house and family was fine or she could question this view, and that might spell disaster. Thus I would make interpretations based on this countertransference and describe to her that she was inviting me to go along with an unrealistically optimistic view of her difficulties and that I had to countenance the threat and the anxiety that disturbing this rosy view would jeopardise her balance, and could even lead to a breakdown.

One day, after a lot of work on this she brought a dream. She was talking to her ex-husband on the phone, simultaneously looking out of the window of her house. Suddenly she saw a sort of aeroplane flying towards it. It was just the back part of a conventional plane but that was how it was designed. It had twin engines on the fins just like the aeroplane that she had gone on with her parents in the 1970s when she was a child. In the dream the aeroplane suddenly crashed into the garden and she said to the husband "Oh, there's a bit of a problem in the garden ... no, it's a disaster!" She said she had been shocked by the dream and then spoke about the fact that the problem of the house was no closer to being resolved. She went on to consider the difficulties: her husband only wanted to pay a very low price for her half of the house but he wanted her to pay much more to him if she was to take over the house. She took a similar stand on the negotiations. This sounded to me like a completely stuck situation but she as she carried on talking she conveyed that it was apparently on the verge of resolution. One thing that she would miss, if he bought her out, would be the garden; it was lovely.

I made a number of interpretations about this. First of all I described how she was now in a state of mind in which there was not really much to worry about: everything in the garden was lovely. However in the dream a different reality had crashed into her mind: it was a disaster. She became very tense and tearful at this point and said that she had recently been thinking about ageing and how the prospect of having children was receding – she became genuinely upset. This did not last long though, and she quickly picked up and got back into "it will be all right in the end" mood. I pointed this out and suggested that this was her means of keeping herself high and that it was a way that she had been using since the 1970s when she was a child: this was her engine. She again became upset and spoke movingly about the hopes she and her husband had had, of building a life in the house and having children. She then herself interpreted another aspect of the dream – the relationship was at its tail-end and it had been a disaster. She then spoke about a feeling that was gathering force in her: a sense of panic that she was approaching the tail-end of her fertility and it might not be all right in the end. Again she was clearly upset and, I thought, very much in touch with the gravity of her situation.

She then began to expand on a complicated analogy about my having helped her leave a safe harbour in order to sail the stormy seas and she was not sure how this would turn out. She developed this further and said that in such circumstances one has to trust the captain of the ship, he has to know the seas and the capabilities of the vessel. As I listened to this I initially felt rather flattered and pleased with myself, clearly she was saying that she experienced me as a competent captain. However I soon found myself getting a little bored and wishing that she would leave this metaphor and I then realised that her mood had changed and she was back in the "it will be all right in the end" state of mind. I interpreted that she was actually currently the captain of our ship and that she had steered us back into the safe harbour of a supposedly helpful relationship. She did not like this and she accused me of ruining her sense that we were making considerable progress, and on this note the session ended.

Discussion

I think this session illustrates how it had become possible to awaken my patient from the soothing illusion that everything would be all be all right in the end. However, it also shows how quickly she would then seek to re-establish her usual defences and would strive to have me collude with them. When I interpreted this it became clear that she felt that I was trying to undermine her.

Betty Joseph (1989) has written that patients enter analysis because their mental balance has been disturbed and then they hope that the analysis can be used to restore their old balance without any further emotional turmoil or expenditure of effort. When the analyst resists this collusive pressure it often becomes clearer that the patient has an allegiance and a loyalty to internal objects who can be powerfully persuasive in the view that the analyst's means of dealing with anxiety is not only inferior to their own but also recklessly dangerous.

When my patient decided to seek out a psychoanalysis for herself because her problems had finally caught up with her, a large part of her unconscious motivation was that she believed that being in analysis would somehow, in itself, offer an escape route from her problems. The analysis was intended to restore the belief that all would be all right in the end because she was in analysis – this was a sufficient condition to preserve the belief that nothing bad had happened, or could happen.

However, when the delusional quality of this belief was repeatedly and convincingly revealed it was not the case that the patient wanted to leave the analysis. In fact her fear then was that I would stop the analysis at that point because I would be unwilling to treat a patient with such unrealistic expectations. I thought at the time that this supported the hypothesis that her major anxiety was about her object's ability to bear anxiety. At this time, while she was very anxious, she also felt very strongly that analysis was vital to her precisely because it was revealing to her the true nature of her difficulties. At this point she asked if she could come for five sessions in the week, and in the third year of the treatment this is what we agreed. It then seemed that a really substantial change in Mrs F was occurring. In support of this view I can cite that at this time she was able to negotiate a deal with her husband which meant that she bought out his share of the house and they finally took the necessary steps to finalise their divorce.

Further material

It was not the case however that there had been a permanent and irreversible change in Mrs F's ways of dealing with difficulties. There began a period in which she repeatedly brought material about her work difficulties and the threats to her position from re-organisation and rationalisation. What was most striking to me was that she was full of anxieties about these proposed changes but, as far as I could establish, made no realistic moves to make her position any safer. For instance she told me about a group of her fellow workers who had got together and were conducting some initial research of their own to demonstrate that the managerial contribution of their work more than offset the cost of their employment. Mrs F made no contribution to this work and claimed that she was constitutionally incapable of such "politicking" and argumentation. Her colleagues' efforts also appeared to demonstrate that a style of management which was more "hands on" was effective – Mrs F felt that this was beyond her. Her efforts were concentrated on making herself as little visible as possible with the hope that she might be overlooked if and when any redundancies were considered.

At about this time Mrs F met a man with whom she established a relationship – I was never to know whether this was a sexual relationship but I did hear that they were spending more and more time together. They both loved walking in the countryside and they found that they had a common ideal: to live in an isolated and beautiful setting far from the urban ugliness of the cities in which they currently lived. Over the space of a few months this evolved into a plan to find a cottage where they could live together "in peace". During this time I made many interpretations about how she was turning away from the research findings of her analysis which revealed that she had to be "hands on" in managing her life and how she found this to be tantamount to living in an ugly place shorn of her beautiful and favoured perspectives on her situation. However I did so with a mounting sense of hopelessness and sometimes felt that it was me who could not face the reality of changes happening which were going to lead to my redundancy. I was particularly struck by her attachment to her new partner who, it seemed to me, shared in and supported her fantasy that there existed a beautiful place from which the ugly realities of the world could be excluded.

I would sometimes think of Freud writing of the use of an "energetic and thorough" procedure to escape reality:

> It regards reality as the sole enemy and as the source of all suffering, with which it is impossible to live, so that one must break off all relations with it if one is to be in any way happy. The hermit turns his back on the world and will have no truck with it. But one can do more than that; one can try to re-create the world, to build up in its stead another world in which its most unbearable features are eliminated and replaced by others that are in conformity with one's own wishes. But whoever, in desperate defiance, sets out upon this path to happiness will as a rule attain nothing. Reality is too strong for him. He becomes a madman, who for the most part finds no one to help him in carrying through his delusion …. A special importance attaches to the case in which this attempt to procure a certainty of happiness and a protection against suffering through a delusional remoulding of reality is made by a considerable number of people in common. The religions of mankind must be classed among the mass-delusions of this kind. No one, needless to say, who shares a delusion ever recognizes it as such.
>
> (Freud, 1930, p. 81)

Thus it seemed to me that, while Mrs F had not been joined by a "considerable" number of people who shared her delusion, her insistence that there could be a place which would be "lovely" gathered much strength when she found a partner who shared this belief. Together they formed a congregation which meant that thereafter she was not substantially threatened by the recognition that this was a delusion.

I also have to admit that it was not completely clear to me that the choice that Mrs F was making was wrong for her. Again Freud on the subject of religion is apposite:

it assures them of its protection and of ultimate happiness in the ups and downs of life ... it satisfies the human thirst for knowledge; it does the same thing that science attempts to do with *its* means, and at that point enters into rivalry with it. Science can be no match for it when it soothes the fear that men feel of the dangers and vicissitudes of life, when it assures them of a happy ending and offers them comfort in unhappiness. It is true that science ... is a powerful helper to men; but there are many situations in which it must leave a man to his suffering and can only advise him to submit to it.

(1933a, pp. 161–162)

Over the next six months or so, in what was now the fifth year of her analysis, I felt increasingly that she was tending towards a decision to move with her partner to a location which would make it very difficult for her to commute to her analysis. She countered these realities by the argument that she and her partner loved to be in the beautiful setting and that this justified all the difficulties a move would create. They began actively to seek a property and eventually found one which was actually in another part of the country and, with enormous trepidation on her part, they committed to its purchase. In the weeks before the final allocation of their funds to the purchase she was enormously anxious but felt that by this time she could not pull out of the arrangement. In this difficult period she often recalled a favourite nursery rhyme about a woman who swallowed a fly. The rhyme continues to describe that she then swallowed a spider (to catch the fly), she then swallowed a bird (to catch the spider), she swallowed a cat (to catch the bird), she swallowed a dog (to catch the cat), she swallowed a goat (to catch the dog), she swallowed a cow (to catch the goat), she swallowed a horse: she died of course! Mrs F would refer to this rhyme and was able to see that she was bound on a course of actions which was intended to get rid of her problems but would in fact compound them. Despite this insight she could not stop herself, and the purchase was completed and she moved away and ended her analysis.

While I was very concerned about her there came a point a few weeks after her involvement with the new man that I knew that she would in all probability end the analysis. It would have been useless to try to resist this knowledge, and anyway I was not

103

convinced that in her case a more realistic confrontation with the reality of her situation was possible; particularly in regard to the terribly painful subject of not having had children. I could not claim with any confidence that her solution to her dilemma of literally fleeing to the other end of the country was a worse strategy than staying in analysis and facing her demons. This was particularly so as in her inner world there was so little support for facing reality, and even meeting five times a week offered little solace compared to moving into a lovely garden.

My understanding of Mrs F's dilemma centred upon her incapacity to feel supported internally as she struggled with doubt, anxiety and depression. It seemed that for a while she experienced the analysis as an external resource that could help her resist the siren call of internal objects who persuaded her not to worry and that everything would be fine. However once these were joined by her new friend's persuasive arguments that together they could create a garden in which everything would be lovely she could no longer resist.

Mr G

I now want to consider the analytic treatment of a patient whose inner world was similarly unsupportive in helping him face reality, essentially because his internal objects turned on him in a cruel and deadly way.

Mr G was in his thirties when I first met him. Two months before I saw him he had made a serious suicide attempt. He had been briefly hospitalised; the psychiatrist who examined him did not think that he was suffering from a depressive illness and discharged him to the care of his general practitioner. He had talked of this experience to a friend who happened to be a colleague of my wife's and she told him she knew a psychoanalyst who he might consult.

My first impressions were of an attractive, well spoken and intelligent man. He told me that he had inherited a substantial amount of money from his parents and that this enabled him to live a dissolute life. He had been unable to maintain any long term relationship, employment or course of study. He had spent much of his adult life fantasising about killing himself, but his recent attempt had been his only serious one.

In the first two consultation meetings I found myself trying to impress upon him that what I offered might be of value to him.

This was partly because I could not imagine that anything other than psychoanalysis might help him, and indeed he had tried many other approaches with little success. However, my opinion was also something of a reaction to the patient's wholesale contempt towards any kind of help. I interpreted this to him, and he agreed that in his view no one could help him but he added, with some insight, that this attitude in itself might be part of his problems. After a prolonged period of consultation in which he insisted that nothing could help him and simultaneously appealed for help, we agreed that he would begin a four times a week treatment. From the outset I was doubtful about this endeavour and began it in a spirit of "Let's at least try, and we'll see what emerges". I communicated this to him in so many words and he seemed appreciative of my clarity.

He is the eldest of two children and his sibling had been successful in life. His parents had died when he was in his early twenties. From the age of about sixteen he had led a very chaotic life. This included promiscuous heterosexual and homosexual sex that was unsafe to the point of being suicidal, periods of severe depression and the abandoning of every effort to develop academically or professionally. His sibling and an aunt were concerned about him and he was both grateful for this and simultaneously resented the fact that they would not let him sink to the depths that seemed to so attract him. He often spoke of a constant refrain of his late mother's; whenever he felt unable to continue with a course of action, she'd say: "Do it for me, darling."

His descents into hopelessness soon made themselves felt in the analysis. Within a few weeks he had despaired of "this form of treatment" being helpful and set himself various deadlines for ending and would then change his mind. At times it was difficult to distinguish between a sense of genuine despair and a more destructive, aggressive and libidinised component. Thus he tried to pull me into feeling hopeless and tried to push me into wanting him to continue his analysis and his life. It was possible to interpret that he was trying to put me in the role of saying "Do it for me, darling" and that in this enactment I was also to carry all the responsibility of the analysis continuing and any hope that it might be helpful. While he could see this and feel genuinely interested in this dynamic he could not maintain his interest in this beyond a session.

I discovered that he had a religious belief and he would frequently speak of a sense of grace that he sought. This concerned a sense of goodness and worthiness and a feeling that God approved of him. It is possible to think of this as a state in which one's internal objects thought well of one, although with my patient it seemed that he sought a state in which his internal objects *only* thought well of him. In fact he gained this sense from his regular meetings with a priest and from a prayer group where his thoughtfulness and religious belief were appreciated. He would frequently contrast this with the "nothing" he got from his analysis.

I will now describe some material from the fourth month of the analysis. There had been a particularly negative period lasting a few days and the patient began a session by telling me he'd met my wife's colleague, the woman who had initially given him my name. She had asked him how the treatment was going. As I listened to this I felt very anxious – what might he have told her? However he did not elaborate but went on to describe meeting a friend's mother. They had been getting on well until she asked him "And what is it you do?" He had blurted out something and tried to cover the shame he felt about having done so little with his life. Five minutes later she had repeated the question. And then the friend's father had come into the room and, on being introduced, asked "And what is it you do?" He told me this was the worst question of all and he dreaded it; it made him feel suicidal.

He then talked about killing himself and his fantasies about his funeral. I found myself imagining attending this and being approached by a stranger who might ask "And what is it you do?" and then having to cover *my* shame about having been the deceased's psychoanalyst. I interpreted that, by telling me about his meeting with the friend who had suggested that he consult me, he had been trying to produce in me a sense of dread about what someone would think about what *I* do. I went on to suggest that he might have imagined that I would be at his funeral and that there too I would have to cope with the dreaded question. The patient confirmed that he had indeed had this thought about my having to justify myself after he killed himself. For a few moments there seemed to be a sense of understanding in the session. One might have imagined that this might have been the prelude to him eventually being able to consider the question "And what is it you do in your analysis that makes it such a failure?"

After a few moments of silence the patient said that he had indeed told this friend about the analysis and that he had done so in such a way that she had apologised to him for having ever suggested that he consult me. This was told to me in a cruel and triumphant tone and shattered my sense that we were in a therapeutic alliance, albeit a temporary one. This was one moment among many in which I got a sense of why the state of grace was so desired: it protected one from a merciless superego that took delight in exposing one's faults pitilessly with no heed of any extenuating circumstances.

In the fifth month of analysis he failed to turn up for two consecutive appointments without informing me. Since he had been talking such a lot about killing himself I became worried to the point of ringing him and leaving a message on his answering machine that I would expect him the next day. He came for that appointment to tell me that he had spent three days in bed with a plastic bag, willing himself to tolerate the agony of suffocation but each time pulling the bag off at the last moment. He told me that he had also lain in the bath for hours with a Stanley knife trying to summon up the resolve to cut his wrists. I felt extreme anxiety on hearing this.

A week later he began a session in the same way as he had begun many others: wondering whether he should continue with the analysis; it was doing no good, surely he should leave. He could only pursue things that "hooked" him; the analysis did not. He went on to describe how the previous day he had been in a pub with a friend who had been captivated by a young blonde barmaid; he couldn't keep his eyes off her. The friend had gone on and on to the patient about how sexy she was and about all the dirty things he would like to do to her.

I interpreted that what really did captivate and "hook" him was the thought of leaving analysis, ending his life, messing everything up. I added that he felt that he could do all sorts of dirty things to me with these thoughts, such as making me so anxious that I had had to ring him when he missed sessions without letting me know why. After a few moments of silence he said "You've identified factor X". He then said nothing else as though the subject had been concluded and I then said that I had been specific in describing something and he had made it mysterious again: factor X. I interpreted in various ways his great difficulty and anxiety about considering what motivated him, paying particular attention to how awful it made him feel about himself.

In the weeks that followed there were occasional indications that the analysis was having some effect. For example, he told me that after he had spent some hours thinking of killing himself, he had rung a friend and told him this and that he had a kitchen knife in his hand. His friend had suggested that he would gain as much if not more pleasure from "sticking the blunt end up his arse" as of putting the sharp end in his chest. He told me this with a kind of wry amusement and agreed with my interpretation that he occasionally allowed me to speak to him about the pleasure he gained from his suicidal thoughts, in a way that he experienced as chiding but friendly. For the most part however I felt his negativity gaining in strength; he spoke more and more of the futility of analysis and the inevitability of suicide.

One Friday there was a very powerful sense of this futility in the session and I described this to him. I remember that at some point in this session I privately comforted myself with the thought that next week would be another week and that we would see how things looked then. It was a means of reminding myself that I was not fully responsible for him and could not know how he would deal with the weekend and it was also a way of freeing myself from this responsibility in order to be able to anticipate enjoying my weekend. All of these thought processes were unspoken but at some point I must have shifted in my seat. Breaking a long silence the patient told me that he had thought that I was moving into a position to deliver a blow to his head in order to kill him. He fervently wished I would do so. I tried to take this up in terms of his despair about himself but with an increasing sense of futility.

No more than a few minutes after leaving the patient rang to say that he would not be returning to analysis. I told him that I would keep to our agreement to hold his sessions open for two weeks, but he was adamant about his decision and kept to his word. When I sent him a bill for the month he sent a cheque for the sessions he had attended with a note saying he was not paying for missed sessions and thanking me for my "services". We had had an agreement that he would pay for missed sessions and for sessions he missed after giving me notice of ending. In not paying for the missed sessions he reneged on this agreement, and I understood that, from his point of view, I was to carry the full cost of the failure of the analysis.

Discussion

I would like to suggest that there were two very important elements in Mr G's relation to the idea of killing himself. Firstly, it was a libidinised idea, he found it extremely captivating and exciting, particularly when it drew in and captivated his object. The material about the friend who tells him where he could stick his knife might indicate some capacity to think about his perverse way of treating me, that is, of keeping me in a dark shitty space while he played with my anxieties. However, when I had interpreted what he was doing, he confounded it by making it factor X.

This difficulty in facing what he did brings me to the second element of his suicidality. His way of leaving the analysis provided a clue: I was to carry the guilt and the responsibility for the failed analysis. I suspect the patient sensed that in that last session I had made a move; not only a physical movement but also an emotional one; I had resigned myself to things being as they were and did not feel that I could be responsible for changing them; all I could do was wait for another week and a change in him. In so doing I might be thought to concur with Freud who argued that the patient's recovery "depends on the interplay of forces in him" (the patient). This freed my patient and me from the "Do it for me, darling" relationship, which I had consciously tried to interpret rather than enact, but which nevertheless was being partially enacted. As I freed myself from this I suspect that the patient was immediately threatened by an unbearable sense of despair, and hence he had wished that I would kill him.

I think that Mr G's way of relating to others, enticing them to wish that he improve and then frustrating them and torturing them, was in itself perhaps a defense against a more terrible situation. I think he believed that it was very dangerous if his people freed themselves from the situation into which he drew them and asked the question "What is it that he is doing?". As he told me, this was the worst question he could be asked because he did not have a God or internal objects who would help him bear knowledge of who he was – he only had a God who could judge him to be full of grace or a God who condemned him unreservedly. Then he feared that then he would be nobody's darling, hated by his people and by his God, and then suicide would become a real possibility. I think that therefore he had to terminate his analysis and attempt to leave the responsibility for its failure at my door.

It is worthwhile considering, however, what responsibility does belong to me and my analytic failure. Did his sadistic libidinisation of wanton destructiveness undermine my ability to maintain an analytic attitude? When I consoled myself with the thought that I could only wait for a change in him was I in fact abandoning him to struggle with a terrible superego and in so doing I was enacting one of its most awful characteristics, namely the way it abandons the self with no support? When he sensed that I had freed myself from a sense of responsibility for him and was preparing to go off for the weekend was he left in a very dangerous and unstable state in which he longed to be put to death? Was his only means of saving himself from this death sentence to put the responsibility firmly in my court?

There is also of course the question of whether I should have taken Mr G into analytic treatment in the first place. Should I have anticipated that the analysis would expose him to danger and should I have made him aware of this risk so that he could have, at least, made a better informed decision about embarking on an analysis? I think the answer to these questions is that I should have done these things but that I was too inexperienced with such patients to have been able to foresee what might happen. In a later chapter I will discuss how very slowly the analyst develops a clinical acumen that is based on accumulated experience. Analytic practice is such that one sees a very limited number of patients. When I saw Mr G I had had a lot of experience of psychotherapy, had finished my analytic training, was running a psychoanalytic practice but I had not hitherto treated anyone who suffered from such a potentially deadly self-appraisal as did Mr G. Faced with the same kind of presentation now I think I would certainly be more able to talk to the patient about how difficult and threatening they would find analytic treatment – whether this would make a difference to what they decided I do not know. It is very difficult to anticipate the dynamic force of events as they unfold in an analysis, and I suspect that most patients cannot imagine how seriously treatment will test their mettle. The same holds true for analysts and even with significant accumulated experience an analyst, if he is being realistic can only begin a treatment in the spirit of "Let's at least try and we'll see what emerges".

6

THE WORK OF SUPERVISION

Introduction

A psychoanalytic aim is to discover a contemporary truth about the relationship that exists in the consulting room. As I have argued in previous chapters, in the circumstances in which the therapist is able to provide and maintain a proper psychoanalytical setting, such a relationship will develop and hence illuminate the patient's means of construing and being in the world and with people. Hence it will provide the material for understanding the patient. However, the clinician's ability to become aware of what is happening in the relationship will be limited by his superego and his ego ideals, as I have shown in previous chapters. In this chapter I will explore how supervision or consultation may enable the clinician to comprehend a little better what is happening and hence enable him to intervene more effectively.

Partly because of my geographical location which for a number of years was largely bereft of psychoanalytic colleagues, and also due to my interest in the development of psychoanalysis in Poland, I have often supervised colleagues who had had very little or no personal therapy. One might think that the supervision of people who had not had the personal experience of their own analysis would present special problems. There are a number of reasons why a reasonably successful personal analysis or therapy should enable a practitioner to function better as a therapist. It should allow the personality to be more tolerant of external reality, and similarly there should be greater acceptance of internal reality. A good analytical experience will lessen a person's need to use omnipotent and omniscient ways of perceiving the world; it

111

should thus decrease the confusion between the actual external world and its distortions by projection. Furthermore, a good analytical experience will enable the person to develop an emotional range and resilience to be able to bear and to accommodate to the difficulties thrown up by external realities. In essence, there will be a lessening of pathological aspects of a punitive superego that does not allow the person to tolerate his or her affects.

However, to recall the observation of Edna O'Shaughnessy which I mentioned in Chapter 1: the patient will consciously and unconsciously monitor the therapist's capacity to understand an issue and will then "pitch" their material beyond that point. They do not necessarily do this to thwart the clinician but frequently in order that their difficulties and their inability to face them can be unconsciously registered by the analyst and thus discovered and thought about and then communicated in words. From this observation one can conclude that the difficulties experienced by therapists who have not had a comprehensive personal analysis will not necessarily differ in kind from those felt by better trained colleagues; in both cases the difficulties they will bring for supervision will reflect a problem in being able to be aware of the relationship that exists in the session and, hence, also an aspect of the countertransference. Later in this chapter I will present vignettes from the supervision of a therapist who had had no personal experience of therapy and from a therapist in training who was in an intensive personal analysis; the process of supervision does not differ radically between them.

My emphasis on the relationship between the patient and the supervisee and the latter's conscious and unconscious countertransference immediately raises the important issue of the differentiation between supervision and personal analysis. Historically this was the fundamental argument between the Vienna and the Budapest training institutes in the 1930s (Caligor, 1981). The Hungarians had instituted what they termed "control analyses" which were in effect the candidate's personal analyst being the supervisor of a third training case, the first and second cases having been supervised by a male and a female training analyst. Sklar (2012) clarified the argument for this practice: normally the countertransference was left by the supervisor to be dealt with in the candidate's analysis, but it was then unknown to what degree it had been successfully analysed. It was argued by the Hungarians that the training analyst would have a particular knowledge of the candidate's personality and history and would thus be particularly prescient about potentially essential matters for the future analyst to understand about himself in relation to his treatment of patients. This third supervision occurred towards the end of the candidate's training, so it was thought that by this time this extra-curricular activity within the analytic relationship would not be too much of an interference in the analytic process. Indeed, it was argued that the "control analysis" could uncover deeper layers of the mind that had hitherto been undiscovered, for instance in the area of unconscious sibling relationships (Sklar, 2012). There is of course a counter-argument: that the practice of the control analysis must have altered dramatically the nature of the personal analysis and confused the clarity of the ending period of the treatment, a time when the problems that an analysand initially brought for analysis may re-appear "with a vengeance!" (Britton, personal communication). The Viennese objected to the practice and argued for a clear and absolute demarcation between personal analysis and supervision, and it is this view which has prevailed in, as far as I know, all current psychoanalytical training programmes.

While the question of the analyst acting as a supervisor has largely been settled, the issue of whether the supervisor should have a conscious therapeutic aim is still very alive. Jacobs (2016), for instance, has argued that "the supervisor at times needs to help the supervisee deal with difficulties in ways that include supportive or insight-oriented therapy" (p. 432). He cited Freud's observation that analysis cannot go further than the analyst's unresolved conflicts, not only to support the view that there is some value in having a case supervised by the supervisee's former analyst, but also to promote the argument that the supervisor should have some idea of a supervisee's personal history in order to be able to make therapeutic links with a countertransferential difficulty. Similarly Berman (2000) wrote:

If we assume that important elements in the transference are relative to the analyst's actual personality and behaviour, it follows that we cannot fully understand the analysand's experience if relevant aspects of the analyst's own personality and emotional reactions are not discussed in the supervision.

(p. 274)

A little later in his paper he gave as an example:

> We need to know ... that the analysand reminds the analyst of her
> brother, if we are to help her in attempting to clarify for herself
> how this association affects her countertransference, uncover the
> ways in which this countertransference unavoidably colours the
> analyst's actions and verbalisations and therefore unknowingly
> influences her analysand as well, changing in turn his transference
> to her and the whole atmosphere in the consulting room.
>
> (p. 275)

I will argue, concurring with Arlow (1963), that a supervision
can be a "psychoanalysis of a psychoanalysis" but should not be a
psychoanalysis of the clinician. Arlow is also clear about what
might be termed a modesty on the part of the supervisor and the
limited effect of supervision in comparison to the personal analysis:
"One can never escape the reality of the situation, namely, that
supervision is essentially and fundamentally a teaching experience"
(1963, p. 587).

There is a lurking suggestion in some of the literature on supervision that a fully trained and well-functioning analyst won't be confronted with unresolved conflicts in his clinical practice. This is
erroneous since the patient will frequently "pitch" his material
beyond the point at which the analyst can readily understand it; the
struggle to become aware of what is beyond one's understanding is
the very essence of analytic work. This phenomenon, of the patient
over time being able to assess the extent of the analyst's ability to
understand and then pitching his material beyond this, means that
the supervisor in his clinical practice has the daily clinical experience
which will allow him to identify with the supervisee's struggle to
come to terms with simply not knowing quite what is going on.
Here I might mention that in Britain at least, in order to be
included in the professional register, every analyst, no matter how
experienced, has to present evidence that they discuss their clinical
work with a colleague or colleagues at regular intervals throughout
the year. These are called consultations; I have often thought this is
to protect the narcissism of those who have long been qualified and
hence do not need "supervision". Although I make light of this, the
understanding that every analyst needs to review his or her clinical
work with a colleague is taken very seriously in Britain.

114

Before I go on to give examples of supervision, I want to consider a concept which is fundamental to my understanding of the supervisory process and to my sense that one can discuss the countertransference with a supervisee without compromising the distinction between supervision and analysis. Sandler and Sandler (1998) made the well accepted (by psychoanalysts) observation that conscious experiences such as dreams, symptoms and sublimations are manifest expressions of latent unconscious knowledge, phantasies and wishes. In their analysis of the way that these behaviours are able both to give some expression to their unconscious origin and, at the same time, preserve some feeling of conscious equanimity, Sandler and Sandler (1998) elaborated the concept of "understanding work". For example, they argued that the dreamer must be unconsciously scanning the dream and unconsciously *understanding* its latent meaning. This kind of monitoring is necessary if the dream is to have performed its function of having some "identity of perception" with, and hence give some expression to, the latent dream wish. (p. 66). The Sandlers applied this analysis to "other surface expressions of unconscious wishes and phantasies". Most importantly they used the concept of understanding work in their analysis of object relationships and described not only how unconscious phantasies are actualised in object relationships but that they are simultaneously understood to have been actualised without this monitoring and feedback ever becoming conscious:

> [T]he individual constantly scans his environment, in particular the reactions of others .... [T]here is a very rapid scanning of the responses of others to "trial" signals or behaviour indications of our own ... we [also] have the capacity to understand, quite unconsciously, the latent meaning of much of what is produced by others .... [O]ur own conscious has to be protected, for we would surely be traumatically overwhelmed if we were to be consciously aware of the latent content of what is manifestly produced and communicated by others.
>
> (pp. 44–45)

To that last sentence one could add "and ourselves, and in our relationships with others".

The experimental work over the last fifty years or so of Howard Shevrin and his co-workers on subliminal priming at the objective detection threshold (summarised and reviewed by Bazan, 2017) has demonstrated the mind's capacity to scan a stimulus, become alert to its latent dynamic significance and then rapidly, almost simultaneously, to activate a defence which ensures that the stimulus, and what it signifies, remain completely outside conscious awareness. That is to say, Shevrin's team have shown the existence of subliminal understanding work and have investigated the neuro-physiological basis of this mechanism of defense. Bazan (2017) clarified that this means of preserving conscious equanimity is a different process from repression, both in terms of the psychological and the neuro-physiological mechanisms involved.

There is another very important aspect to the concept of understanding work. It is often the case that the unconscious understanding presses for some kind of expression; indeed, one can argue that this is the underlying rationale for the method of free association and its corresponding consequence for the analytic approach of paying close attention to all aspects of the patient's communications. Freud (1905) wrote of Dora that she was unable to keep her wish to masturbate a secret since she betrayed it by the way she played with her reticule. As well as a betrayal one might also think of an unconscious need in her to give expression to what she unconsciously understood; this might be thought of as a corollary to, or an expression of, an epistemological instinct. Thus, so often patients can describe very accurately the clinical situation, as they see it, in an unconscious communication. There is both an unconscious communication of what is understood to be going on and an unconscious apprehending by the other; this ability is common to the clinician and to the patient.

The Sandlers' concept of "understanding work" has been largely ignored in the analytic literature but I think it forms a fundamental basis for an approach to supervision. It not only provides the means of understanding better the means by which "the *Ucs.* of one human being can react upon that of another, without passing through the *Cs.*" (Freud, 1915b, p. 194). It also means that in the material brought for supervision there will be the means for understanding what is going on at an unconscious level, in the treatment. The focus will of course be on the patient's material, but if the supervisor insists on the clinician bringing process notes then, in the creation and reporting of them, the clinician will convey his own unconscious working over of the session, his own understanding work, which the supervisor may be able to discern. Arlow (1963) put this very well:

116

The gaps in the record lend an air of ambiguity to the therapist's report. This element of ambiguity has a function in the supervisory experience which is similar to the role of ambiguity in the aesthetic experience. It provides an opportunity for the supervisor to fill in the gaps with his own understanding of the patient, of the therapist, and of the interaction between the two of them.

(p. 588)

I will give two examples of supervision, the first taken from the supervision of a colleague who had not had an analysis or a comprehensive psychoanalytical training and the second from the weekly supervision of an experienced psychoanalytical psychotherapist who was completing her training and who was concurrently in intensive psychoanalytical treatment.

Supervision one

This material is taken from the supervision of a therapist who is an experienced clinical psychologist, with no formal psychotherapy training but with a wealth of clinical experience and a personality that inspires trust and respect in his patients and colleagues. He was working, in a once a week therapy, with a fifty year old woman who had been the victim of sexual abuse by her father following her mother's death when she was seven. The patient had led a difficult life that had included a marriage to an emotionally and physically abusive man. However, she had extricated herself from this and after a number of further sado-masochistic relationships she came for therapy. At the time she felt she needed help in consolidating a new relationship with a man who seemed kinder and more supportive than her previous partners. The patient had had the insight that there was something in her which could ruin this new relationship unless she received help.

From what my supervisee had gathered the patient had been much closer to her father than to her mother, and they appeared to have enjoyed a good non-abusive relationship before the mother's death. After his wife had died the father seemed to have suffered a depressive breakdown and, on his return home after a period of hospitalisation, father and daughter shared the marital bed until the patient was in her early teens. The therapy had reached a point at which the patient was exploring memories of

117

having received emotional comfort from the physical contact with her father. As far as the therapist was able to gather they had engaged in mutual petting without there having been penetration. She had suggested in a recent session that she might have been ambivalent about her mother's survival.

At the point the therapist brought the case for supervision the patient had become clinically depressed, had begun to neglect her appearance and was jeopardising her work and her new relationship. She had spoken of a feeling that the sword that she felt had been hanging over her for all of her life was about to drop. The therapist had tried various interpretations that did not improve the situation and he had become very worried about the patient. He resolved to change his approach and to talk to her about how she might cope better with her depression. He also said to her that he would discuss her case with her general practitioner and would suggest that she begin a course of anti-depressants. However, the patient had become more depressed and began to complain about the treatment and the awful situation it had brought her to.

A dream was the central point of the session that the therapist presented. The patient had dreamt that she was in a room from which she could see through a doorway into an adjoining room. She became a little anxious as the light in her room began to fade and eventually it went out. She could still see because some light came from the neighbouring room. However, the dream became a nightmare as the light in that room faded, and she had woken in an extremely anxious state as everything went black. She had one association: she attended evening classes in which participants tried to trace their family histories. She thought the teacher was excellent but a difficulty had arisen. The caretaker of the school where the class was held did not want it to continue because it meant he had to work late and he had started to turn off the lights before the allotted time. The teacher, a kind and gentle man according to the patient's portrayal (also an apt description of the therapist), seemed to be intimidated by this man, and the patient had tried to find ways of supporting the teacher in standing up to him.

As the therapist and I discussed this we formulated the problem in the following terms: that throughout her life the patient had dealt with her guilt about the death of her mother and the subsequent abuse by the masochistic solution of colluding in bad treatment of herself. She was now trying to break this pattern and live in a better relationship with her new friend. She sensed however that her unconscious guilt would not let her do this and she had come for therapy to try and resolve this. As she reached that point in the therapy at which she had to consider what the causes of her guilt were, and also, of course, as she felt herself in the transference to be in a relationship in which she received relief and comfort, she had panicked. And, crucially, so had the therapist to the extent that he had tried to work in a different way. The patient had understood this as evidence that her guilt was unmanageable and had become extremely anxious about the depth of her depression.

I thought her dream symbolised this dilemma. The caretaker could be seen as a punitive superego who throughout her life had taken care to ensure that she was badly treated. It now threatened her with the ultimate punishment, suicide, the lights going out before the allotted time. Her dream showed that she could bear this anxiety if the light in the neighbouring room stayed on. That is to say, if her therapist, the kind teacher who was helping her find out about her history, was not overwhelmed by anxiety and could in some way stand up to and shed light on the bullying and intimidating superego. All this she could dream but her capacity to dream broke down when she sensed that the light next door had been extinguished, the teacher/therapist had been intimidated by the bully, and then no further thinking or dreaming could go on.

Discussion of this understanding formed one important part of the supervision session but I also used the material to speak to the therapist about the superego and its pathological manifestations. I spent a significant amount of time talking to the therapist about the emotional strain that the patient had imposed upon him. I introduced this by saying something like:

> This is a really good example of just how difficult it is, particularly I think when one is quite experienced and hence feels that one really does carry clinical responsibility, to deal with the unspoken threat that the patient might kill herself. I think in such a situation it is quite likely that we lose our faith in interpretation and try to find other means of helping the patient. But I think it is very important to try and resist this temptation and to keep trying to think about what one's countertransference might mean. There is no easy solution, this is seriously difficult work emotionally.

This led us on to talk about just how threatened he had been by this case and he told me how he had come to dread her sessions and to think that he might be ill on the day that she was due, thus ensuring that he would have to cancel their meeting. He also disclosed that he had had fantasies that he would hear about the patient's suicide and then of how he would be blamed by her relatives and shunned by his colleagues for being such an inept therapist. He had imagined that he would lose his professional reputation. This enabled us to elaborate how important it was to understand this very difficult countertransference as a communication about the patient's own superego and the way it had treated her throughout her life.

In the session following the above supervision the therapist found an opportunity to say to the patient that he thought she had really wanted him to understand how frightened she was when she thought about what had happened in her childhood; she could feel so guilty that she feared she would kill herself. He added that she had tried to get him to feel this fear in order to have it understood. In response to this the patient said that she had been thinking increasingly about killing herself. Crucially, the therapist felt at that moment that this was told to him not as a threat, but as a communication of an anxiety that the patient wanted him to understand. That is to say, the therapist had been restored as someone who she could communicate with about her anxieties. Some capacity to think had been restored. Her dream had detailed exactly at what point she felt she had lost this neighbouring, functioning, mind, and it is interesting to note that it was exactly then that her capacity to dream had broken down.

Of course, this was not the end of difficulties in this case, and he continued to bring the case for supervision over the next two years. Other difficulties arose but the patient did eventually marry her partner. Their relationship continued to be disturbed by her attempts to pull her husband into sado-masochistic ways of relating but there was some development of an increasing capacity to contain this inclination and to talk to her husband about it in order to enlist his help in stopping her attempts to ruin their marriage.

Throughout the supervision of this case I would frequently talk to the therapist about his countertransference and the emotional pressures that treating this patient subjected him to. Most clinicians would have been made very anxious by such a presentation; indeed, if they did not become so, then they would have been missing a vital communication. However, I also imagined that there must have been personal historical reasons in the therapist's background which made him particularly susceptible to this presentation. For instance, he reported that he imagined that he might be ill on the day of this patient's session; many therapists would instead hope that the patient might be ill and have to cancel. He seemed to be particularly prone to a sense of persecutory guilt which suggested that he had not sufficiently suffered a conscious awareness of his sadism. I did once say to him that it was somewhat unusual that he had hoped that he would be ill rather than the patient but I did not enquire further into this during the supervision. I left it for him to think more deeply about this, if he were able and willing to do so.

It might have been tempting in such circumstances to blur the distinction between supervision and personal therapy by enquiring into the therapist's background, especially as I knew that the therapist was not in personal therapy and hence had no formal setting in which to do this kind of exploration. This might be the kind of situation in which Jacobs (2016) or Berman (2000) would advocate this sort of intervention. To my mind this kind of approach confuses supervision with personal therapy or analysis. Inevitably the clinician will have contributed personally to what is happening in the therapy. I have tried to illustrate that one can explore the relevant dynamics as they appear in the clinical situation without actually going into the personal details underlying the therapist's contribution.

I have always avoided any enquiry into the personal backgrounds of my supervisees and have not felt disadvantaged by doing so. This does not mean that I do not take into account what the clinical work means to the therapist personally, and I will now give another example which will illustrate this.

Supervision two

This therapist was also a clinical psychologist but she was formally training to be a psychoanalytic psychotherapist and hence she was in an intensive personal analysis. She had had some difficulties in the training in that she had assessed a number of previous patients before successfully engaging one in treatment. That was her first case, and when she was ready to take her second case, under my supervision, there were similar problems. Finally, a man of thirty who was complaining of depression following the break-up of a relationship began three times a week treatment. The patient had a history of very difficult relationships and he had come for treatment after the last of these broke down and he had begun to feel depressed. He was physically attractive and quite successful professionally as well as being a gifted sportsman. He had had numerous brief relationships but whenever one began to become serious he panicked and finished it. Alternatively, his partner would finish it because she became fed up with his lack of commitment. He began his therapy by giving the therapist a list of dates he would not be able to manage in the first few weeks of the treatment.

Early indications were of a narcissistic man who used his attractiveness to be seductive but who also played a cruel game of getting his girlfriends to desire him and then treating them badly and meeting with them only on his own terms. This could be understood as a means of defending himself against the vulnerability of being rejected himself, and it was possible to link this with abandonment he had suffered as a child. He had been rejected by his mother who herself had been abandoned by his father who he had never known; he had been adopted and brought up by his strict maternal grandparents. This kind of understanding, of his having to provoke a feeling of rejection in others, was premature to be used in interpretation in that it was only intellectual. The emotional problem that was uppermost in the treatment was, as one would predict, that the patient, although knowing that he needed to undergo treatment, was unable to commit himself fully to it.

This supervision session is taken from very early on in the treatment, from the sixth week to be precise. As we began the supervision I asked how it had been going generally. The therapist said it was going OK but that she was still worried about the treatment. I said that this was natural since it was very early on and the task was still one of trying to help the patient settle into the therapy, and we knew that committing himself was his primary difficulty. The therapist agreed with this but added that there were times when she felt very inhibited with the patient. She felt this was due to her anxiety about keeping him in treatment but there were times when she thought the patient did something that made it hard for her to think and interpret as she would wish. She then told me the session she had brought.

122

The patient was ten minutes late and apologised saying he had been to his physiotherapist; he had recently suffered a bad sporting injury to his back. He had had a very bad night, his back pain had been awful, he had had some reports to write but could only sit for fifteen minutes at a time, he felt he was crumbling, his spine did not feel it could hold him upright. The work of writing the reports had not gone well, it was something he would usually do without any difficulty but not now. The therapist told me that at this point she had wanted to say that she thought he was telling her not only about the back problem but also about how difficult and painful he was finding it to be in therapy; that it felt to him as though the way he had managed in the past, which had served as his backbone, was crumbling leaving him unable to function. However, she told me that she had felt curiously inhibited about making this interpretation and had stayed silent.

The patient had gone on to describe in a much more cheerful way how well he was thought of in the last company he had worked for. There was still talk there about what a good salesman he had been, there were myths about the deals he had pulled off. He then told quite a complicated story. In essence it concerned a man who worked for an organisation that bought the products of the company the patient had worked for. The patient had reason to believe that this man had been infiltrated into that organisation by a rival firm in order that he could put lucrative contracts their way. This was to the detriment of the patient's firm. As I listened to this story I found it improbable but then thought that perhaps such shenanigans really did go on in big business. The patient was wondering whether to expose this publicly but feared the repercussions that might follow.

The therapist tried to take this up in terms of how hurt the patient was by this trickery and how difficult he found it to accept this hurt part of himself. The patient agreed and said that he always tried to pass his pain off as a joke but, he added thoughtfully, this might be because he was never sure if he was wanted unless he was successful. This was said movingly, but the patient quickly moved on to describe a colleague who had been talking to him about a difficulty at work but who, when the patient had used the word "problem", had said: "Don't call it a problem, it's defeatist."

He went on to describe a job he might apply for in London. When he had been down there to investigate this possibility, he had been invited to an exclusive London club. The rest of the session was spent in describing the wonderful luxurious fittings of this club and the famous clientele he had mixed with, and the therapist reported that she felt unable to intervene in any effective way up to the end of the session.

As I listened to this account one of the first things that struck me was the thought that if the patient were to get a job in London then he would have to abandon his therapy, in the North of England, and I was surprised that the therapist did not seem alive to this. I was also struck with the fact that the therapist had been able to formulate a good interpretation (about the way that the patient felt his defences were crumbling and that what had served as his spine or backbone was not able to support him any longer) but had felt unable to give it. She had been able to make other, less telling, interventions.

I spoke to her about the interpretation she had not given and said that I thought it had been right and that one could see other material in the session that supported it. For instance, there was the patient's colleague who said that even using the word "problem" was defeatist. I said I thought that the patient at critical parts of the session functioned as though this was his belief too. For instance, after he has spoken of his physical pain and his feeling of crumbling, he had immediately gone on to say what a great salesman he was and how wonderful people thought him to be. The same pattern was evident later in the session when the patient talked movingly about fearing he might not be wanted unless he was successful; particularly poignant as he had really not been wanted by his mother. He had quickly moved on from this to talk about being in a very privileged place, the London club, and had left the therapist feeling left out and unwanted. I did say at this point that I was surprised that she had not realised that his going to London would mean that his therapy had to end. She was shocked by this and said that it had not even occurred to her and that of course it would mean that. Thoughtfully she then said that she was probably so anxious about the possibility of this happening, given how difficult she had found it to establish patients in treatment, that she had been unable to think about it.

I was not sure how to take this further and went back to elaborating what I thought was the main theme of the session, that is, the patient's difficulty in tolerating psychic pain. I said I thought that he used his own means of trying to deal with his pain and

124

that there was an element of competition with the therapist about this. I thought this could be seen in the early material of the session in which he had described the competition between the two companies. The therapist said she thought this was right and that from the beginning of the therapy there had been an unspoken rivalry between them: between what she offered and the way that the patient wanted to deal with his problems. That is to say, she had felt that the patient, while asking for her help, also believed that psychotherapy was a useless treatment compared to his way of dealing with depression, even though that had failed.

We were now able to see how the material about the competition between the companies was a metaphor for what was going on in the transference–countertransference matrix. I said I thought that we needed to consider carefully the patient's idea that there was an unscrupulous firm who were unethically trying to win business for themselves. I then suggested to the therapist that there was a way that this applied in the treatment situation and that I thought this was inhibiting her ability to interpret. I said that she was understandably very anxious that this patient might not be able to settle in treatment and that she would lose him. Part of this anxiety was ethical, that is to say, that she believed that this form of treatment was right for him. But there were other feelings she had which did not have the patient's interests as central and were more concerned about her need to have a training patient who stayed the course. I put this in a very careful way and tried to make it clear that I thought this was absolutely normal and to be expected in her situation. But I thought that this need in her made it very difficult to distinguish between trying to engage the patient in treatment for his benefit and trying to do so for hers. I suggested that this dilemma had inhibited her in pursuing the right line of interpretation; she had got worried that she would be trying to drum up business for herself in an unethical way.

The therapist reacted with relief to this and went on to say how she did need to be able to own her need for the patient to attend and that this was indeed a difficult thing to acknowledge. We went on to discuss how this might be made more difficult by this particular patient and his great sensitivity to whether his object really wanted him. We then spoke about the patient's wish to expose somebody as unethical and how the patient in the transference would wish to bring into the open his anxiety that his therapist would be trying to undo his defences in order to win business for herself. We concluded that an effective interpretation would be that he feared that this was her aim and that she would take retribution if he exposed this anxiety to her.

Near the end of the session the therapist told me that this was all connected with personal issues for her. I acknowledged that this might be the case but I said that an ordinary and understandable professional anxiety of keeping her training patient and the effect this had on her work was what we could discuss.

I have wanted to show that it can be possible at times in super-vision to discuss the dynamics of the patient as they manifest them-selves in the session and also to discuss the countertransferential difficulties that are raised during the work. In many cases of course the two are connected in that the countertransferential difficulties are a tremendous block to the therapist being able to see what the dynamics are. Thus, the therapist feared that if it were disclosed in any way that she needed her patient for her own reasons then she would be revealed as unethical and would lose her patient. This anxiety was so disabling that she turned a blind eye to the fact that if the patient moved his work to London he would have to ter-minate his therapy. By uncovering this anxiety in the supervision the therapist was helped to become more open inside herself to the fact that she needed her patient. This in turn enabled her to distinguish between her selfish wish for the patient to stay in the treatment and other more concerned and reparative wishes. She then felt less guilty and was able to explore more with the patient his phantasies about her.

I want to underline that it was not necessary to look at the par-ticularly personal reasons behind the supervisee's anxiety. The patient's material was quite sufficient to understand all that needed to be understood in order to clarify the atmosphere in the session and to begin to resolve it so that something of an impasse could be overcome and its dynamics understood. I also want to underline that the impasse was produced *primarily* by the patient's pathology of always wanting his object to want and desire him. The fact that he was able to use a particular professional pre-occupation of his therapist which had a more personal genesis is entirely incidental; if he had not managed to create this countertransference in this way he would have done it by another means. Indeed in the following months he regularly did so. As her supervisor I did not need to concern myself with the exact nature of the personal contribution made by the supervisee to the analytic relationship; that was for her personal analysis, if she decided to take it there. My responsibility was only with spelling out the nature of the current relationship in the therapy.

This material also is intended to illustrate understanding work, in this case the remarkable capacity of the patient unconsciously to understand his therapist's pre-occupations. The patient's material about the rival firm, who may have been unscrupulously trying to win business for themselves, not only conveyed his suspiciousness about his therapist but it also, to a degree, disabled her from seeing what he was doing and then interpreting it. To some degree the supervision was helpful in freeing her from this paralysis.

Conclusion

Since Searles (1955) published his classic paper on the informational value of the supervisor's experience, several authors have noted how, at times, an issue that is alive in a case brought for supervision can also be experienced in the supervisory couple. This has become known as the parallel process (Doehrman, 1976). Brenman Pick (2012) described a consultation in which she had observed that her supervisee's patient was trying to compromise his professional behaviour. At the end of the consultation the supervisee offered to pay her in cash in such a way that this immediately brought the issue of her professional standards into focus: would she declare the earnings to the tax authorities? I know from personal experience that focusing on identifying such a parallel is not Brenman Pick's primary means of doing supervision. While I have sometimes become aware of this kind of parallel enactment in my own work as a supervisor it is also not my principal method of trying to understand; such parallels are illuminating when they happen, but one cannot base one's whole supervisory approach on their occurrence.

I would like, however, to draw attention to the ubiquitous parallel between all participants in the relationships I have been discussing in this chapter. They all feel under scrutiny: the patient, the trainee, the qualified analyst and the supervisor. They all have the potential to feel that they have failed to meet the aspirations of their various ego ideals and then to be attacked by a damning superego. As I argued in Chapters 2 and 4, these potentialities never disappear, and the therapeutic relationship, with its scrutiny of personal actions and their meanings, so often brings them to the fore. The most common parallel process is based upon the similarity between the patient's anxiety of how he will be evaluated by the analyst and the supervisee's anxiety about the supervisor's assessment of the quality of the work. This anxiety of being judged can also apply to the therapist's fear of being judged by the patient as in my second example. The supervisor too can feel anxious about the supervisee's assessment. The anxiety raised by scrutiny is most clearly seen when the supervisee is in a training and the supervisor carries the responsibility of assessing their credibility as a potential analyst or therapist. My experience suggests that this anxiety is little different when the supervisee is not being reported upon; there is still a fear of being judged. Arlow (1963) indicated this parallel process and anticipated my central argument when he wrote:

> Strachey is of the opinion that the major cause of the mitigation of the neurotic conflict may be traced to the shifting balance between the various functions of the psyche made possible by an alteration of the superego. This modification, he says, takes place through an unconscious identification with the superego functioning of the therapist. A similar set of forces operates in the supervisory situation.
>
> (1963, p. 590)

I do not think that the process of supervision can change the severity of the superego – what it can do is to alert the supervisee to the restrictions imposed by the superego and the consequences thereof. This is akin to what Britton (2003) described as the emancipation of the ego from the superego, but which I think can be more accurately described as a more benign superego supporting the ego against the accusations of the pathological superego.

I have not experienced much inhibition on the part of the supervisee in relation to the fact that, if they are training, they know that I will be writing six-monthly reports on their work and progress. I do take the attitude that we are colleagues, considering difficult material, and that I am in a privileged position because I am at one remove from the patient, the supervisee has already done some understanding work in unconsciously processing the material in order to bring it to supervision, and I have a greater range and depth of experience.

In a geographical setting in which one is the only analyst and many of one's supervisees are not in analysis it might be tempting to mix up the role of supervisor and analyst. By not doing so I do not think that I disadvantaged my supervisees – indeed I believe that their knowledge that I would not use an opportunity to delve into their private matters enabled them to be more open about the emotions and thoughts that clinical work stirred up in them. A good supervisory experience, that is, one that respects the limitations of supervision as I have described, can provide the therapist with an opportunity to think about their personal contribution to the difficulty of discovering what is happening in the here and now of the session. And that, in turn, can be an opportunity for professional and personal development.

7

CONSIDERING OTHER APPROACHES

Introduction

Poland (2009) explored what might be the underlying factors that make for the difficulties experienced when psychoanalysts from different schools discuss their approaches and the commonly observed outbreaks of hostility and even "ridicule" (p. 250). He particularly identified a threat to one's narcissism as something that exacerbated "the politics of identity" and a descent into hostility towards other groups (p. 251). He argued that this is very difficult to avoid since our subject matter is so complex and any one viewpoint is hence incomplete, making challenges to one's narcissism unavoidable.

In Chapter 4 I discussed the analyst's narcissism indirectly in terms of the ego ideals to which the analyst aspired and I distinguished between an ego ideal that takes pride in discovery of what approximates to the truth and an ego ideal that seeks to cure and I described how these might sometimes be in conflict. Poland centred his argument on the former aspiration and described the competitiveness amongst psychoanalytic colleagues and schools that stems from wishing to be like Freud, a conquistador of new knowledge (p. 252).

Poland convincingly showed how the inevitable failure to be omniscient can lead to a compensatory sense of superiority and then:

The air of superiority spreads broadly. It is evident in collegial consultations when a supervisory tone replaces mutual respect (Gabbard, personal communication), and it appears in our literature when a writer's own thinking, presented in its greatest strength, is contrasted with contrary views presented in their weakest light. Our debates are rife with such straw men.

(pp. 253–254)

I would add to Poland's argument the motivation that comes from a failure to achieve the demands made by what I called the depressive or reparative ego idea. I once heard Elizabeth Spillius say in a clinical seminar that clinical responsibility weighed heavily on clinicians and could be one of the pressures that drove them into groupings where their clinical approach could be apparently justified by group membership. An underlying sense of unconscious guilt and shame about having failed a patient can be a factor in the passions generated when matters of technique and approach are discussed and can form a largely unacknowledged aspect of the occasional descent into what Smith (2003) has referred to as "epistemological warfare" in which rival factions go head to head. An inkling that one's treatment of a patient has been less than the best possible seriously threatens one's sense of wellbeing, a state of grace in which one feels that one's internal objects approve of and support one. Hence to question another clinician's approach or to have one's own questioned always runs the risk that the ensuing debate will create more heat than light.

Much depends on the spirit in which the discussion is held and a continuing awareness that while discussion of difference is vital to a discipline it will also raise anxieties. The level of apprehension is raised considerably when there is an implication that a different approach, while maybe therapeutic, is not psychoanalytical, with the implication that its practitioners are not psychoanalysts; this immediately raises an intense disquiet about excommunication or exile (Blass, 2010a, 2010b). While it is theoretically important to try to delineate what distinguishes psychoanalysis from other psychological treatments, history suggests that it is almost impossible to do so practically without exciting hostility. So much is at stake: not only professional standing but also a sense that one has fulfilled one's duty to the patient to have delivered a psychoanalytical treatment.

There are other inherent difficulties in discussing theoretical approaches which are not one's own. In an editorial of the *International Journal of Psychoanalysis* Birksted-Breen (2010) explored the parallels between the analyst's task of translating the patient's material in all its various manifestations into an interpretation, and the translator's task of transforming words and meanings from one language to another. The latter is in some ways an impossible task since a word in one language will carry a plethora of meanings and associations which a word in a different language cannot convey, however close its dictionary definition. So it is with the analyst's task: no matter how precise he tries to make his interpretation it cannot convey the full meaning of the patient's material whose original form is overdetermined and its meanings multiple. Birksted-Breen described these limitations in the analyst's work as a context for considering the difficulties in comparing differences in theory and technique between psychoanalytic schools. Both theory and technique are embedded in a surfeit of context, connotation and culture, and without a deep immersion in a particular milieu it is somewhat foolhardy to offer comment or critique. And yet if one assumes that psychoanalysis is a scientific activity, in the broadest sense of being an attempt to articulate the truest possible account of its subject matter, and then test its assertion against experiential evidence with rigour, then comparisons across psychoanalytic cultures are a necessity. Comparison and critique may broaden understanding and allow the consideration of a wider range of relevant variables than had previously been possible, while enabling the exclusion of those which are not justified by clinical evidence.

In the more formal sciences theory can be tested by experiment which seeks to replicate the original findings which supported the theory. Psychoanalysis does not enjoy this possibility. The raw data of psychoanalysis is clinical material which can never be replicated, and its reporting and evaluation are in themselves problematic (Ward, 1997). Nevertheless when clinical data is reported it immediately invites from the reader a consideration and analysis of its validity; indeed Spence (1997) has argued that the practical measure of the validity assigned to theory is in direct proportion to the interest it excites from the analytic community. While this is troubling, since it may mean that psychoanalytic theory and technique are prone to fashion, it is likely that more well established sciences are not immune to this.

Smith (2003) has argued that the signifiers which denote affiliation and theoretical differences "probably reflect very little of how we actually work, and they most assuredly have lost all meaningful specificity". Waelder (1962) distinguished different levels of descriptive specificity, moving from a report of clinical observation, to clinical interpretation of the material, then to clinical generalisation and on to clinical theory (pp. 619–620). It is to the latter two levels that discussion of differences between schools of psychoanalysis tends to gravitate and thus suffers from the problem outlined by Smith. An examination of differences between approaches is more likely to be fruitful, albeit still likely to stir up anxieties and perhaps "epistemological warfare", if the comparisons are made at the level of clinical observations and clinical interpretation, always bearing in mind Widlöcher's (2002) remark that "I do not expect clinical practice to enable us to transcend differences … it is these very differences which help us to make progress." He too noted how frequently participants in the debate of difference strayed from an optimal level of discourse: "Between a dogmatic teaching and a pugnacious proselytism there was often little room for authentic debates" (p. 210). On a more optimistic note Bernardi (2008), describing the healthy development of psychoanalysis in the Rio Plate region, noted that "privileging the clinical level of the discussion facilitates dialogue between different psychoanalytic cultures" (p. 207). I have observed a similar development in the British Psychoanalytical Society in the thirty or so years I have been a member.

Having noted the potential pitfalls of discussing differences in approach, I am going to discuss the clinical work of other psychoanalysts in as much as they relate to the main thesis of this book. The authors whose work I am going to examine are eminent proponents of their particular approaches and, in the particular publications I will consider, they have given, not only a full description of their clinical work, but also a generous and detailed description of the analyst's countertransference.

Before I consider contemporary psychoanalytic approaches I will examine a historic case of Freud's which illustrates some of the issues I wish to discuss.

The Wolf Man

On 13 February 1910 Freud wrote to Ferenczi:

> A rich young Russian, whom I took on because of compulsive tendencies, admitted the following transferences to me after the first session: Jewish swindler, he would like to use me from behind and shit on my head. At the age of six years he experienced as his first symptom cursing against God: pig, dog, etc. When he saw three piles of faeces on the street he became uncomfortable

133

because of the Holy Trinity and anxiously sought a fourth in order
to destroy the association.

(Freud 1910a, p. 138)

The patient of course came to be known as the Wolf Man, probably
the most famous of all psychoanalytic cases. His hostility was immediately apparent in the transference to Freud and in the history of
his symptoms. Gay (1988) noted that from the beginning of the
treatment there was an air of aggression and hostility felt by Freud
in relation to this case, not towards the patient but rather to two of
his previous therapists, Theodor Ziehen and Emil Kraepelin, both of
whom Freud felt to be his rivals for academic acclaim; both had previously failed to help the Wolf Man. And Gay suggested that the
publication of the case, in 1918, partly because of delays caused by
the Great War, was in part an attack on Jung for downplaying the
importance of sexuality in the aetiology of mental illness. But it
would seem that Freud was unable to locate the issue of hostility in
the transference and in the countertransference and instead, I will
suggest, acted it out under the guise of introducing a technical
innovation.

The treatment lasted four and a half years and was ended by
Freud setting a deadline for its termination. Even within the report
of the case, Freud (1918) counselled against such a procedure:

> Of the physician's point of view I can only declare that in a case
> of this kind he must behave as "timelessly" as the unconscious
> itself, if he wishes to learn anything or to achieve anything. And
> in the end he will succeed in doing so, if he has the strength to
> renounce any short-sighted therapeutic ambition.
>
> (p. 10)

In reality Freud was unable to follow his own advice. Gay (1988)
described the circumstances (quotations within the text are to
Freud's paper):

> [The treatment's] difficulties were more conspicuous than its
> fruitfulness. "The first years of the treatment brought scarcely
> any change." The Wolf Man was courtesy itself but kept himself
> "unassailably entrenched" in an attitude of "submissive indiffer-
> ence". He listened, understood, and did not permit anything to

touch him. Freud found it all very frustrating. "His unimpeachable intelligence was as if cut off from the instinctual forces that governed his conduct." The Wolf Man took untold months before he began to participate in the work of analysis, and then, once he felt the pressure of internal change, he resumed his gently sabotaging ways. He inevitably found his illness too precious to exchange for the uncertain benefits of relative help. In this predicament Freud decided to set a termination date – one year hence – for the analysis, and stick to it inflexibly.

Although at the end of that period both analyst and patient judged the procedure and the analysis to have been a success, Freud later acknowledged that his treatment of the Wolf Man was only partially successful and that his patient continued to struggle and had several more episodes of serious mental illness in his life (1937, p. 218).

Freud (1937) understood these recurrences of illness as being due in the main to "pathogenic material ... of pieces of the patient's childhood history which had not come to light when I was analysing him". However, in the same paragraph Freud wrote: "Some of these attacks were still concerned with residual portions of the transference; and, where this was so, short-lived though they were, they showed a distinctly paranoid character" (p. 218). Freud's emphasis in 1937 was still on a particular aspect of the childhood sexual history. While he may have initially been fascinated by the transference he described to Ferenczi in 1910, by 1914 he was unable to tolerate what we might call the daily shitting on his head, the anal intercourse of the taking in of his interpretations into a place that rendered them impotent; one might even go as far as to suggest that it was the Wolf Man who was the swindler, accepting Freud's efforts to help him but not repaying Freud with a sense of clinical achievement. Thus what Freud did not explore in the transference/countertransference was a different childhood and infantile history (of which Freud was not unaware): that of a destructive narcissism which attacked the parental function, particularly the father's, and in turn Freud's analysis, and in consequence would have left the Wolf Man in a paranoid state of mind, fearing retaliation. In his short analysis with Brunswick (which on Freud's instruction was offered without a fee) his destructive narcissism was much more to the fore of the analyst's attention and interpretive intent, but the Wolf Man countered this by an insistence that she was a poor substitute for Freud, presumably thus making his analyst feel that it was she who had a problem with injured narcissism (Gardiner, 1983). His paranoia in relation to Freud can be understood as a persecutory guilt about what he had done to Freud's efforts to help him (Meissner, 1977). To my mind, Freud did give an indication of his countertransference to the Wolf Man when in 1937, in advocating sticking to a set termination date he wrote: "the lion springs once and once only" (1937, p. 219). The lion of course springs with murderous intent.

This is not to say that the analysis with Freud did not help the Wolf Man at all. He was married for thirty years, until his wife's suicide; he was able to do some professional work; he retained an interest in a cultural and intellectual life; he painted and he wrote. But in the latter part of his life he was involved in a long relationship with a very disturbed and demanding woman who ruthlessly exploited him financially. Gardiner (1983) who knew the Wolf Man for over fifty years, understood this relationship as providing the Wolf Man with a purpose in a life that would otherwise have felt empty, but the relationship is also open to the interpretation that it was a form of expiation of the Wolf Man's sense of guilt about the way he himself had exploited other people. For many years he was financially supported by the analytic community, initially on Freud's initiative, and had several more analytic treatments (Roazen, 1979). His assessment of the help he had received from Freud was not in terms of having received a better understanding of himself but rather that:

> the most important thing, when I came to Professor Freud, was that he agreed me going back to Therese [who became the Wolf Man's wife] which I later did. Had he been against, I would surely not have remained with him.
>
> (Gardiner, 1983, p. 875)

This suggests that while the Wolf Man was undoubtedly helped by Freud's interest and support, and in later years that of other analysts, he did not judge that the help was of a psychoanalytic nature. Freud was unable to analyse what we would now call the Wolf Man's destructive narcissism; even though he was aware of it, he did not analyse its effect within the transference:

He fell ill, therefore, as the result of a *narcissistic* frustration. This excessive strength of his narcissism was in complete harmony with the other indications of an inhibited sexual development: with the fact that so few of his psychical trends were concentrated in his heterosexual object-choice ... and that his homosexual attitude, standing so much nearer to narcissism, persisted in him as an unconscious force with such great tenacity. Naturally, where disturbances like these are present, psychoanalytic treatment cannot bring about any instantaneous revolution or put matters upon a level with a normal development.

(1918, p. 118, Freud's italics)

While I am aware of other related perspectives on Freud's treatment of the Wolf Man (e.g. Blum, 1974), the central point in my view is that the case can be seen as an early example of the analyst being affected by the patient's hostility and responding to it, not by analysing it in the transference, but by introducing a technical parameter: in this case, the enforced termination of the analysis.

Relational psychoanalysis

In 2007 I was privileged to be a discussant to a paper given to the British Psychoanalytical Society by a leading proponent of relational psychoanalysis, Jessica Benjamin. Relational psychoanalysis is a clinical approach which has gained a large following in North America and elsewhere. This discussion later featured in the series of Psychoanalytic Controversies in the *International Journal of Psychoanalysis* (Benjamin, 2009a, 2009b; Blass, 2009; Sedlak, 2009). After discussing Benjamin's contribution, I will consider aspects of the psychoanalytical school from which relational psychoanalysis developed (Brandchaft et al., 2010), namely self psychology, and consider the approach of its practitioners to the issue of hostility in both the patient and the clinician.

In her presentation to the British Psychoanalytical Society, Benjamin argued that in the course of a treatment there are likely to be misunderstandings which will repeat the hurts of the past and which she called ruptures in attunement. My understanding of the main point she wanted to make was that the clinician's acknowledgement of having caused such hurt is a restoration of what she called the moral third, which I understood as a relationship in which truthfulness, respect for the other and faith in the process of being

137

recognised were foremost. She argued that without such an acknowledgement the patient may experience the analyst as an impervious, omnipotent "mother-as-god" and as the same "as the original abuser or bystander adult [who] denied the child's reality" (2009a, pp. 443–444).

The material she presented to illustrate her argument was taken from a session towards the end of a long analysis. The female patient wearily told her analyst that she could not be bothered recounting the repetitive dreams she had had yet again about being inferior to her colleagues. She then recalled a film she saw the previous evening: it starred Nicole Kidman and was entitled *To Die For*. Kidman played the part of a glamorous and murderous woman who exploited a younger girl who had been molested and "forever neglected" and who adulated the Kidman character. The patient said that she laughed raucously during the film but felt increasingly weird and disorientated. The analyst asked about this and the patient said that she identified with the younger exploited woman who had been a terribly unhappy teenager.

Benjamin then recounted that throughout the analysis the patient had been masochistically beating herself up (which was indicated in the dreams she could not be bothered to report) while at the same time portraying her analyst as the perfect, idealised Kidman-like figure. However this picture did not tally with the analyst's counter-transference which was described as: "perhaps a joint defence against my playing the sadistic part – that of the frustrated helpless witness who can do nothing" (p. 445). At this point Benjamin expanded on her understanding of this and its significance in relation to the patient's history. She described how she would feel that she was either trying to deny the patient's negativity, leaving the patient to face a catastrophe and her shame about it on her own, or she could empathise with the patient's utter dejection and then the two of them would be in mutual despair. She understood this as a failure that replicated the mother's inability to be a soothing mother who heard the baby's distress but was not immediately identified with it. She was able to move out of this position when she was more able to confront the patient with her part in the repetitive self beating: "your lack of compassion toward you" (p. 447). She described this in her presentation as "an emotionally authentic response" and an example of a "moral third" that respects human vulnerability. That development, which occurred relatively early in the analysis, could nevertheless be regularly negated, and the patient would return to her self-beating and self-disparagement.

Benjamin then described "an important enactment" which she used to make her point that self-disclosure was a means of repairing the rupture that occurs when the analyst fails to be "the complete container". The patient had again returned to self-disparagement about herself as a mother, and the analyst failed to contain her frustration and said that she wondered whether the patient would carry this propensity to denigrate herself into her relationship with her children. The patient replied "That was Draconian" and then immediately tried to rationalise her analyst's perceived sharpness as a relational attempt to help her; she was, after all, a relational analyst. The analyst stated that the patient should not let her off the hook so readily and should hold her to account for her sharp riposte and she admitted her difficulty in listening to the patient turn herself into a failure again. In the discussion of this vignette Benjamin described her realisation that she had become identified with the pathetically inadequate mother. However, she argued that the episode was transformative in that her acknowledgement of her mistake demonstrated "a sense of solidity" which enabled the patient to "develop her own sense of agency and responsibility". She concluded "Such action is meant to show that the analyst *can* change, can model the transformational process, and that revealing her struggle to do so also transforms the analytic process into one of mutual listening to multiple voices" (p. 450). She implied that this modelling and the patient's experience of being in a mutually shared process in which rupture can be repaired by acknowledgement of shame and guilt was transformative and restored the moral third.

In my discussion at the Scientific Meeting at which Jessica Benjamin presented her paper, I argued that while we might agree that lawful relating which recognised one's own and others' subjectivity is a worthwhile aim of psychoanalysis, I thought we disagreed strongly on the means of achieving this. The presented patient had clearly made very worthwhile progress in her life during her long analysis in terms of becoming a successful professional, a partner and a mother. However, she regularly engaged in vicious bouts of self-hatred in which she demeaned herself in comparison to her more successful and attractive colleagues and friends. I understood the clinical approach to this to be based on an understanding that the patient's mother was uncontaining and could not help the patient process her unhappiness, her neediness and her disappointment in herself. Lacking such a container the patient was not able to deal with her self-doubts in any way other than to dissociate herself from them and then indulge in shameful and masochistic beatings. The analyst's aim in such a situation was to provide a container for the patient's sense of unworthiness in order that she would be able to re-connect with her shameful and bad self in a more contained, and hence a more concerned, humane and moral way. A central feature of such containment was the demonstration that the analyst herself could contain and acknowledge her own shame about having acted badly. This provided a modelling, for example, of being able to survive scrutiny.

I suggested that a different perspective would be to see the patient as being caught up in a sado-masochistic pattern in which she is both the beater and the beaten. I thought that one could take this view further and hypothesise that the patient got a very particular and perverse pleasure from this. One could interpret then that she was identified not only with Nicole Kidman's victim but also with a murderous Nicole Kidman and that unconsciously she idealised this identification but could not give thought to it; hence the raucous laughter and at the same time a growing sense of dissociation. To make use of the title of the film: this way of treating herself and her object is *To Die For*, i.e. she did not care that in indulging this part of herself she did indeed kill the creative work she and her analyst had done. From this perspective the analyst was not just a hapless bystander as the patient beat herself up; the analyst was the victim.

After the analyst snapped she stressed the need to acknowledge her lapse, apologise for her sharpness and suggest that the patient should not let her off the hook. I suggested that another way of looking at the situation was that the analyst's sharpness was an unmediated (albeit understandable) response to having her work and achievements murdered yet again. The analyst in her sharp rejoinder pointed out to the patient how damaging to others her behaviour is. Essentially she told the patient that it would be destructive to the patient's children if they were forever confronted with a mother who felt badly about herself, presumably and understandably because it would make them feel that they themselves could not mitigate their mother's continuing unhappiness. I took this to be an example of a commonly observed phenomenon: the analyst is able to describe the patient's destructiveness but not in relation to the analyst in the transference, but rather with someone else as the victim.

The essence of my argument was that the approach that Benjamin advocated and illustrated scotomised the main transferential–counter-transferential dynamic. I did not wish to minimise the difficulties presented by the case and I could see that if one were to take up the patient's sadism and her delight in it, in a more direct way, then the patient could feel blamed, held responsible, shamed, and this could easily lead to the sort of rupture or impasse that Benjamin wanted to avoid. I argued that there could be several reasons for such impasses but I wanted to focus on two in particular. The first was that in such a situation the analyst did indeed convey some sense of blame or disappointment in the patient. However, this would stem from subscribing to a moral sense of how things should be, i.e. fair and lawful, rather than a more psychoanalytical view-point which held that frequently humans did not behave in that way, and then had to struggle, in various ways, with the conse-quences. As I have argued throughout this book this a difficult thing for the analyst to do: to remember that it is the patient's prerogative to be as she or he is, but it is the analyst's responsibility only to describe this, not to make a moral judgement of it, which is almost inevitably the first lens that one spontaneously uses (like/dislike, approval/disapproval). If one can be aware of this spontaneous judgement and really struggle to master it then this sometimes com-municates itself to the patient, and they are then able to reflect on themselves in a more contained way. I argued that the analyst did not need to acknowledge her faulty and moral stance prior to undertaking the process of working through in the countertransference, a process which would allow a more effective containment of a moralistic viewpoint. Indeed such acknowledgement, to my mind, was in itself dubious – had the analyst lost faith in the patient's ability to observe her and draw her own conclusions? The danger in acknowledgement may be that the patient feels that the analyst needs to establish herself quickly as the good and moral object. This may even be understood as the analyst not being able to struggle for long with guilt.

This brought me to another difficulty since, in my experience, when one does address the patient's sadism and perversity then it is often the case that a very malignant object comes into view. Some-times, as I have described, it is the analyst's superego and the way that the patient has drawn out the analyst's insistence on morality. Even when this has been "tamed", so to speak, in some cases this is not the end of the problem; something in the patient remains very active and

141

stops analytic progress. This might be due to the severity of the patient's superego, they do not deserve improvement, or it might be due to their inability to give up the sublime pleasure they take from their perversity. The analyst can only struggle to describe the exact nature of the bad object, but sometimes an analysis breaks down in these situations, as I described in Chapter 5.

I ended my discussion by strongly agreeing with Jessica Benjamin that the analyst's constant scrutiny of him- or herself was a vital part of the analytic process. This is a part of a Socratic self-questioning which is essential. It is at its most vital when the analyst questions whether he is being analytical, that is, striving to describe what is happening truthfully and without moral condemnation. It could even be argued that the best safeguard of morality is a striving to understand the clinical situation from this psychoanalytical viewpoint rather than from a moral perspective.

Self psychology

My discussion with Jessica Benjamin prompted my interest in the development from which relational psychoanalysis traces its origins: Kohut's self psychology (Brandchaft et al., 2010). Self psychology fundamentally divided the worldwide psychoanalytic community on grounds which are particularly pertinent to the points of view advanced in this book. I will briefly review this controversy in the history of the psychoanalytic movement and then consider some of Kohut's arguments for the change of direction he took when he created this different theoretical and technical approach.

While it is acknowledged by the psychoanalytic profession that the discipline has become what Wallerstein (1988) in his presidential address to the International Psychoanalytical Association termed "pluralistic", it is disputed by some commentators whether the plural theories espoused by the different schools do actually translate to substantial differences in clinical practice. In his two presidential addresses to the IPA, Wallerstein (1988, 1990) stated that when one examined actual clinical material from analysts who came from very different theoretical backgrounds and geographical areas there was "common ground" in what they actually did. He argued that this made for a common psychoanalytic identity, and what characterised clinical work that could be termed psychoanalytical was a focus on what Sandler and Sandler (1984) had termed the present unconscious.

Wallerstein considered that the schools of psychoanalytic thought he discussed in his presentations all focused on understanding the current emotional situation in the consulting room and based their interpretations to the patient upon this understanding. Such analytical activity encompassed core psychoanalytical principles such as the transference, the dynamic unconscious, conflict and unconscious phantasy, all *sine qua non* constructs employed by the psychoanalyst which identify him as a psychoanalyst.

Wallerstein (1988) cited an extract from Kohut's (1984) last book in which the author gave a detailed account (in Kohut pp. 92ff) of an interchange with a Kleinian colleague from Latin America. She had described a session which followed her having told her patient about an unexpected cancellation of an imminent session. The patient had, in the following session, been withdrawn and uncommunicative and eventually the analyst had interpreted that the patient now experienced her as a rejecting and cold bad breast and that the patient both expressed and guarded against her sadistic and aggressive response by becoming silent and inhibiting her oral sadism, which would otherwise be expressed by "biting words". The interpretation, which Kohut described as being given in a warm and understanding tone of voice, led to a change in the atmosphere of the session and allowed the patient to give further material which was analytically useful.

Kohut argued that an alternative interpretation given by an American ego psychoanalyst might have stressed the Oedipal aspects of the transference and would have described the patient as feeling like a child, abandoned by a mother who had joined the father in the parental bedroom from which the child was excluded. He then gave another alternative interpretation, this time the kind of intervention that a self psychologist would have made. This described to the patient that with the loss of a self-sustaining self-object the patient was left feeling empty, not fully alive. (Self-object in self psychology is defined as an objectively external object which is used by the subject to support the cohesion of the self.)

In Wallerstein's opinion all three alternative interpretations equally conveyed that the analyst understood that the "the patient was sorely troubled over the announced cancellation and was understandably reacting unhappily to it" (1988, p. 14). To my mind this was true only up to a point; there remained a fundamental difference between the Kleinian and classical interpretations on the one hand, and the self-psychological interpretation on the other. The difference lay in how closely the interpretation corresponded to a hypothesised truth about the patient's feelings towards the analyst, precisely in relation to the issue of hostility. Both the Kleinian and the ego psychology interpretations described the analyst being experienced as an object who was hostile to the patient: "bad" or "abandoning" or "excluding". And, in turn, both interpretations suggested that the patient had to guard against her own hostile and destructive responses: the "biting words". This is in contrast to Kohut's own suggested interpretation which emphasised, not the presence of a bad object, but rather the absence of the good sustaining object, the self-object; in the absence of this self-object the patient's sense of self disintegrates because the experience "repeats the traumatic unavailability of the self-confirming responses in early life" (Kohut, 1984, p. 102).

Wallerstein (1988) himself partially acknowledged this difference:

> I include in this conception of who and what is properly psychoanalytic Kohut's self-psychology even though it avows itself to be centrally a psychology of the supraordinate self and its developmental struggle for cohesion, with a psychopathology and a therapy based on conceptions of deficit and of restoration rather than primarily of conflict and its resolution. I do this on the basis of my reading of the clinical material presented by Kohut and other self psychologists and my view of the clinical data that are presented.
>
> (1988, footnote p. 12)

Whether one judges Kohut's development to be within or outside the field of psychoanalysis is not, at this moment, relevant to the discussion; the essential point is that the formulation of the aetiology of pathology and the way of understanding the means by which a treatment can help to ameliorate suffering are both fundamentally different. Self psychology minimises to a large extent the primary importance of infantile hostility conceptualised as an inherent drive provoked into expression by frustration. Its focus is much more on the ability or otherwise of the caretakers to help the infant modify and contain its hostility when faced with frustration, thus enabling development in conditions of optimal frustration.

In order to examine these differences further, to relate them to my thesis and to understand more deeply why Kohut developed self psychology as an alternative approach, I will consider Kohut's retrospective view of his treatments of Mr Z given in his 1984 book. He wrote that in Mr Z's first analysis, his understanding of his patient was based on a theoretical orientation which saw his patient's narcissistic demands as "a clinging to narcissistic infantile gratification". This, he wrote, meant that his interpretations tended to have "at least a trace of rejection and censure" (p. 90); at this time he interpreted as if "these outdated drive-pleasures ... must be opposed by the reality principle *and the strictures of adult morality*" (p. 84, my italics). He was able to escape such moralising and censure when he shifted his theoretical focus and saw his patient's demands as a more reasonable request/need for experience which would lead to greater maturity and which had previously been frustrated by mis-attuned self-objects. Kohut wrote:

> If the analyst sees the infantile eroticism and aggression that emerge in the analysand's transference as in essence fuelled by primary infantile drives that are being re-activated, he will respond to them in a different way from the analyst who considers them secondary, symptomatic manifestations and looks at the undernourished self as the locus of the primary disturbance. However softened by the compassion and tact of the analyst, interpretations of infantile seductive and aggressive behaviour ... will be experienced by patients as subtly censorious and disapproving.
>
> (pp. 90–91)

Kohut was aware that his previous approach had been experienced as critical and, while Mr Z had largely submitted to it, this, Kohut later understood, was largely due to compliance and masochism and was in part a function of the maternal transference. In the original paper he had written:

> Put most concisely: my theoretical convictions, the convictions of a classical analyst who saw the material that the patient presented in terms of infantile drives and of conflicts about them, and of agencies of a mental apparatus either clashing or co-operating with each other, had become for the patient a replica of the mother's hidden psychosis, of a distorted outlook on the world to which he had adjusted in childhood, which he had accepted as reality – an attitude of compliance and acceptance that he had

now reinstated with regard to me and to the seemingly unshakable convictions that I held.

(Kohut, 1979, pp. 15–16)

Thus, Kohut acknowledged to himself that this was not only a displacement from the past but that he had indeed been critical and moralistic. This despite feeling sympathy and patience and striving to remain neutral. One can only admire Kohut's bravery and open-mindedness in facing this truth about the first analysis; his realisation of how he had behaved may be the first published account of the countertransferential difficulty that is this book's main subject matter.

As I have shown in previous chapters, clinicians have to be aware that the danger Kohut described, of being censorious, is a very real one and one that is difficult to avoid: as Fajrajzen (2014) described, the compulsion to judge is almost ubiquitous and so often is the first perspective that is taken. However, it need not be an inevitable one, but in order to keep it in check psychoanalysts not only have to elaborate their theory of change but they have to work consistently on their countertransference: to the patient, to psychoanalysis and to themselves as a psychoanalyst.

The views of pathogenesis and cure are radically changed in Kohut's theory: the pathology is due to a failing in the original self-objects; the analyst will be a different self- object, a more empathic one, and this will allow the patient to develop a more cohesive self. Moreover the adoption of this theoretical outlook will free the analyst from having to struggle with his moralistic judgement: "the self psychologically informed psychoanalyst blames no one, neither the patient nor his parents" (Kohut, 1984, p. 25). One might dispute whether the approach really does not hold the original caretakers responsible for later pathology, but what is clear is that Kohut believed that the self psychology approach, if applied correctly, could free the clinician from a personal struggle with the issues of blame, guilt and shame.

In my opinion, if one looks at the actual reported work of some of the relational and intersubjective psychoanalysts one can see that in striving not to be critical or to assign blame they have also had to curtail their critical judgement. My discussion of Benjamin's paper above was intended to demonstrate this point. Another example is given by Brandchaft et al. (2010) who described a most

146

provocative and trying patient who insisted that the analyst must not show the slightest hint of irritation or frustration in the face of his non-attendance or his withholding the analyst's payment over many weeks. In the face of this the analyst reported how he came to admire the patient's absolute insistence on being himself and not abiding by the rules imposed by others. Is this humanly possible without scotomising one's feelings of resentment and critical judgement? Most analysts could only manage this by assuming a saintliness only achieved by denying their true feelings. This might protect against the potential danger of destructive acting-in on the part of the analyst, but it might well be at the expense of fully experiencing the countertransference and hence using it as a potential source of analytic working through and elaboration.

Kohut maintained that it was after he shifted his theoretical stance from classical psychoanalysis to self psychology, he was able to have a more real contact with his patient's rage and aggression (1984, pp. 137–139). One would imagine that this would mean that these feelings would be reflected in the countertransference, thus requiring a difficult and demanding task of containment from the analyst. However, Kohut wrote in the same work (p. 81) that analysts practising self psychology:

> tend to work in a more relaxed fashion, are more easygoing with their patients, have fewer misgivings about making themselves emotionally available to their patients if the need arises and generally behave in a (comparatively speaking) less reserved manner than the majority of analysts.

I would concur with Caper (1999, p. 285) who understood this greater flexibility and ability to be more easy-going in the following way:

> By the time Kohut undertook Mr Z's second analysis, his approach had changed significantly. He was able to demur from the coercive tactics that had formed such an important part of the first analysis. This was clearly a substantial technical improvement, and one that brought obvious and justified relief to both patient and analyst. But now Kohut, having abandoned a technique that unintentionally encouraged the patient to split off something bad into his analyst, began to encourage the patient to do the same thing with his mother. He took at face value the patient's

assertions that his psychopathology must have stemmed entirely from his mother's destructive frustration of his healthy attempts to develop. This technical stance was another way of encouraging splitting in the patient. It prevented both analyst and patient from exploring the patient's own contributions to his difficulties, either with his mother or in his first analysis. Kohut's approach interfered with the patient's being able to integrate the destructive aspects of his own personality.

Within the British Society in the thirty years that I have been a member, I have observed what might be called a softening of the approach taken towards patients; it might more accurately be described as a growing awareness of the narcissistic vulnerability that being a patient entails. John Steiner's (2011) contribution was a case in point and illustrated a sensitivity to patients' problems with shame and embarrassment as well as with guilt. However, to my knowledge few analysts in Britain, with the possible exception of Mollon (1993), have, like Bernardi (2011) in Uruguay, acknowledged Kohut's contribution and its integration into their own approach. My impression is that rather than viewing Kohut as providing a necessary balance between scientific rigour and empathic identification, most British analysts would agree with Caper (1999) that a necessary consideration of destructive aspects of the patient and its consequences for the patient is lost in Kohut's approach. However, I would guess that many would be sympathetic to his sensitivity and honesty in addressing the difficulty of "moderating the harshness which truth can sometimes evoke" (Steiner, 2013).

As I noted in the introduction to this chapter, the discussion about differences in approach can so quickly extend into matters which arouse great anxieties, foremost in these and implicit in Wallerstein's presentations is the question of "What is psychoanalysis?" and almost always closely followed by "Who is entitled to call themselves a psychoanalyst?". Then a very moralistic tone prevails and anxieties about excommunication or being seen as beyond the pale come to the fore.

When the European Psychoanalytic Federation's workshops on Comparing Clinical Methods were set up, a guiding principle was that participants were required to consider that the work presented *was* psychoanalysis and this was not to be questioned. By explicitly banning the question "Is this psychoanalysis?" the instigators of these workshops tried to avoid generating too much of the anxiety that surrounds the comparison of clinical methods. They were successful on the whole in creating a setting in which colleagues could discuss clinical material in depth in a mutually respectful atmosphere (Tuckett et al., 2008). However, a critical reading of a later contribution from Tuckett (2011), in which he reviewed his experience of the workshops, suggests that this judgement about what the analyst is doing and whether it is psychoanalytical or not, is ubiquitous. In his later contribution there is a strong suggestion that on further reflection he considered that some of the technical innovations introduced by the psychoanalyst, who described their clinical work in the workshops, fell outside of what *he* would consider as psychoanalytical. Their intent was to provide a patient with a "safer" or "better" experience than the analyst supposed they had suffered in a traumatising past; his observation was that many psychoanalysts now believe that their clinical efficacy is based on their ability to provide their patients with a "new" experience. In a footnote Tuckett wrote that this effort to provide a "good enough relationship" was frequently linked to "disenchantment with interpretation" (p. 1386). He suggested that, without intending to practise a self psychology or relational approach, the type of intervention often observed in the European workshops might be a consequence of the analyst having been pulled into an adaptation to the patient's emotional demands. In such situations the analyst would forgo an examination of the transference–countertransference relationship and its links with the patient's history and pathology, and instead try to provide an ameliorative experience. He warned (2011, p. 1367) that this has resulted in a situation in which "psychoanalysis as practised today is in danger of losing its specificity and so losing its way".

Rangell (2008) was able to reflect on over fifty years in the vanguard of American psychoanalysis and in his review of its history he clearly demarcated a split along the lines which are associated with the issues I am discussing: between "the neutral, that is, objective analytic attitude, or the 'corrective emotional experience'" (p. 223). Like Hanna Segal (personal communication), Rangell argued that of course a good analysis should be a corrective emotional experience and that the split could have been mended in the 1950s in the States, were it not for personalities! I would add that the personalities are under the sway of the ubiquity of hostility which quickly becomes moralistic and then impedes integration and the dispassionate discussion of difference.

To summarise: I have tried to show that while Kohut identified the important issue of the analyst's unconscious moralistic attitude and its detrimental effect upon the patient, in my view he mistakenly attributed this to the theoretical stance of the analyst. I have argued that this did not make for freedom from moral judgement – his approach has resulted in the original caretakers being held responsible for the patient's pathology. While this provided a necessary reminder that the qualities of the object are important, both in history and in the consulting room, in my view this understanding went too far in scotomising a patient's hostility and destructiveness. I have also tried to show how discussion of these issues can itself be ambushed by hostility which provokes a moralism and can lead to an atmosphere in which condemnation and the threat of excommunication invade discourse. My purpose has not been to recommend a solution to these difficulties in discourse but to suggest that they arise, at least in part, when practitioners are threatened by a sense that they have not sufficiently fulfilled their clinical responsibilities.

An approach based on the analyst's intuition

Rangell (2008) and Poland (2009), both of whom have the wisdom and farsightedness of elder statesmen and have offered long-ranging retrospectives of psychoanalytical history, warn of the dangers of a *pars pro toto* application of new theories and insights. A certain theoretical and technical approach is developed and is then applied comprehensively to all clinical phenomena thus apparently scotomising all previous approaches and understandings. I wish to discuss an example of this phenomenon which also illustrates my thesis that the analyst will find a particular difficulty in considering the patient's hostility. I am aware of the danger that I will be seen to be advocating a *pars pro toto* application of my viewpoint.

The detailed clinical material I will consider comes from the French analysts César and Sára Botella (2005). Their contribution is based upon clinical experience which would appear to suggest that the patient suffers from a deficit of symbolisation; that is to say, the patient is unable to represent the emotional forces and conflicts that govern his behaviour, and as a consequence the

150

analyst has to find in himself a representation, a means of symbolising the dilemma. A number of authors, quite independently have similarly stressed that with at least some patients it is the analyst who has to be able to find or intuit a means of representing the hitherto unmentalised depiction of what is happening emotionally within the analytic session.

In the United States, Ogden (e.g. 1994) introduced the concept of the analytic third to describe a shared fantasy created mutually by patient and analyst which the analyst can intuit by considering the "here and now" relevance of his (the analyst's) free associations. One instance he gave is that of finding himself in a session thinking that what he had thought to be a personal letter might have actually been sent to a much wider audience; later in the session he thought that he would have to hurry to collect his repaired car from the garage; he found himself feeling angry that the garage owner shut his garage punctually at six pm even though Ogden was a long-time customer and the garage owner knew he really needed his car. From these thoughts Ogden discerned that his patient felt that his analyst was working mechanically and impersonally. He was able to put this together with his countertransference feeling of frustration that he could not make better contact with his patient and also with the patient's sense that something vital was missing in his relationships with his wife and children. Ogden was also reminded that the patient had described his mother as "brain dead" and having no sense or empathy with his emotional state. He employed these insights in an effective interpretation which radically changed the mood of the session. In his work Ogden has stressed the importance of taking seriously such apparently random thoughts and that the analyst can use these to orient himself to what is going on in the session.

In Britain Birksted–Breen (2009, 2012, 2016) and Perelberg (2015) have advanced the most comprehensive theoretical and technical arguments about the central necessity for the analyst's reverie. Birksted–Breen, like the French writers cited below has focused on the appearance of a "sudden and often fleeting visual image" which gives expression to a quality which had hitherto lacked representability. "[T]he pictorial representation may need to take place *in the mind of the analyst* when it cannot take place in the mind of the patient, via a regressive state" (2016, p. 36, my italics). She gives examples of such images: in one instance, as she decided that a usual way of interpreting would only lead to her and her patient taking up their "usual positions" and hence would herald an impasse, she stayed silent and then she "had a powerful visual image of someone underwater, adrift in the open sea after the rope holding a boat to a rock has broken" (2012, p. 828). As the patient was speaking of not having something solid to hold on to (the analyst had recently cancelled some sessions) she said "Like a rock". This eased the atmosphere and the patient then spoke of a warmer interaction with his family and contemplating having a child with his partner. In her 2016 paper she described a "hallucinosis" in which, while looking at her patient's coat on an armchair in her consulting room, she "saw": "a lion or panther lying on its haunches and looking straight at me. ... The beast was there on the chair for a few sessions and then disappeared as mysteriously" (pp. 32–33). A little later in the analysis the patient brought a dream in which he was in bed with his wife and a lion was asleep with its head weighing heavily on the patient's shoulder while a cheetah observed him from the floor of the bedroom. This led to further analytic work and a lessening of the patient's obsessive intellectual defences. In this example the analyst did not make use of her visual image (of the wild cats) in an interpretation but she argued convincingly that her state of reverie, which allowed her to "hallucinate", created a setting that eventually enabled the patient to create his dream.

A number of analysts have been inspired by the later work of Bion with its emphasis on "O" and its clinical recommendations of an attitude of "no memory, no desire, no coherence, no understanding" (Vermote, 2011, p. 1089). They have argued that this approach allows for the analyst to be able to enter a state of reverie in which he may be able to access an approximation to a representation of the patient's dilemma which would otherwise remain unimagined and un-depicted. Ferro (e.g. 2009) has based a similar way of working on the contributions of Baranger and Baranger (1961–62 but printed in English in 2008) and their theory of the psychoanalytic field, together with his understanding of the later work of Bion and he has argued in many papers that the analyst must be able to dream what the patient is unable to dream.

Although based in a different theoretical system the work of a group of French analysts has also described a way of working which focuses on the analyst's ability to find representation in his mind for experiences which, they have argued, the patient is unable to represent and to experience emotionally. De M'Uzan (e.g. 1976) described the necessary state of mind of the analyst as a depersonalisation, and more recently Ithier (2016) has described the fantasy or pictogram that the analyst may experience as a "chimera". She draws comparisons between this way of working and those described by Ogden and Ferro. Also in France, Botella and Botella (2005) have called the process by which such phenomena are created "the work of figurability". They too have argued that this is the means of achieving a representation of that which has hitherto been unrepresented. It is dependent on the analyst being able to abandon him/herself and join the patient in a formal regression (akin to de M'Uzan's concept of the analyst's depersonalisation).

In South America this thinking has found expression in the work of Rocha Barros and Lieberman (2000) who use the term "affective pictogram" to convey the analyst's experience of an image or memory or dream that is then elaborated into an understanding. Some analysts working in this tradition such as Botella and Botella (2005) consider it important that the analyst, emerging from his/her regressed state, is able to elaborate verbally an understanding of their intuitive sense. Others (e.g. Vermote, 2011) believe that it is sufficient for the analyst to articulate an image or an association and that this can be sufficient in facilitating further elaboration/development in the patient. (See Vermote (2011) and Taylor (2011) for a fascinating discussion of this point.) Birksted-Breen (2010) commented that such an approach attempts to construct a language where none was thought to exist previously, but whether it is really the case that the patient had no means of representation is itself is a view I will attempt to challenge in the latter part of this chapter.

Largely because they give a full account of a session together with a detailed description of the analyst's various countertransferential states during it, I am going to examine the work of the Botellas. Although they do not openly state that the analyst may need to dream the patient they do argue (2005, pp. 67–68) that the work of figurability is akin to "dream work" and most importantly they make the bold claim that their approach allows a deeper access to the unconscious than does an examination of the transference–countertransference matrix. They also do not use Bion's term of reverie but employ the concept of the double to depict the process that the analyst has to allow in order to reach the required depth of understanding. Thus, "functioning or working as a double", the analyst is able to transform what they consider are traumatic experiences which cannot be represented ("weak spots … flaws, gaping holes in … functioning", p. 71), initially by either party, into psychic experience which can be subjected to thought.

The patient they presented to illustrate the work of figurability is male, as is the analyst. He presented with "an apparently normal neurosis" but at times of stress he used means of coping "other than those characteristic of neurosis" (p. 71). For instance, he was constantly observing the analyst and would cling to these perceptions not, the authors argued, in order to avoid the emergence of repressed ideas but "as a means of survival against the disorganising effect of losing his perception of the analyst" (p. 72).

Prior to the reported session the patient brought a rare dream in which he and the analyst were together, the analyst went into a shower and the patient didn't follow him. In the commentary on this dream the authors suggest that it might be understood as an indication of a developing disinvestment of a homosexual identification with the analyst. At the beginning of the next session, the patient reported that that morning he had seen the analyst in the street. The analyst had in fact been taking a walk with his wife, something the patient did not refer to throughout the session. When the analyst did not respond to this, the patient became uncertain about whether he had actually seen the analyst and became increasingly tense, asking the analyst anxiously for instance whether he had been wearing dark glasses in the street. The analyst meanwhile began to feel a "derealisation" stemming from the discrepancy between *his* memory of a nice morning walk with his wife and the "embarrassing" portrayal given by the patient. He also began to be "infiltrated" with thoughts about dark glasses, the word "hieratic" (which means solemn or rigid) and then went on to think of a character from the film of the living dead. At this point, the authors argued, this thought was a product of a regressed dream state which contrasted drastically with the relaxed sense of his morning walk which was a function of his "diurnal ego". The analyst then tried to make light of the nightmarish version of himself by humour: he thought of himself as a corpse on holiday, but this did not alleviate for long his "terror". Meanwhile the patient said "I don't know any more if I saw you … I am looking for you in the image and I can't find you any more" (pp. 72–73).

In their commentary the authors contended that the analyst's "nightmare" of himself as one of the living dead was the product of a "work of figurability". And then they went further: the analyst's nightmare was a response to the patient's negative hallucination (not finding the analyst in the image).

The patient then reminded the analyst of the dream about the shower from the previous day, and the analyst was relieved to turn his mind to that and away from his "nightmare". The patient then began to talk about his work at a hospital and three deaths that had occurred, one of them of a Holocaust survivor. In his mind the analyst immediately linked the shower to the gas chamber and realised that the dream was not about being able to resist a longing for a homosexual relationship, but rather about not wanting to follow the analyst into death. Rather strangely the authors then report "the analyst heard himself saying: 'The shower is a gas chamber'" (p. 74). This intervention led to violent sobbing by the patient which continued to the end of the session. The authors argued that this was the echo of the affect which had hitherto been foreclosed in him but which had found expression in the analyst's nightmare.

In offering an alternative understanding of the clinical material I am not intending to argue for a more comprehensive or a superior approach. Instead it is to challenge the view that the approach which stresses the need for a formal regression in the analyst, so he can do the work of figurability, is itself superior to other approaches, which stress the close examination of the transference–countertransference matrix. My intention is to show: a) that the concept of unrepresentability in the patient and hence the need for the work of figurability on the part of the analyst is not supported by the clinical data and b) to offer a suggestion of why the analyst needed to regress in the way described.

My argument begins with consideration of what the authors call the patient's negative hallucination: the patient says "I don't know any more if I saw you … I am looking for you in the image and I can't find you any more." If one takes this, not as an inability to represent the analyst and his wife, but as an annihilation of an image that invoked in the patient a murderous hatred, then the session can be seen from a different viewpoint. The analyst's nightmare is of being one of the "living dead"; a reference to a film genre in which "reanimated human corpses … feast on the flesh and/or brains of the living" (Wikipedia). That is to say the analyst's nightmare would be to realise that the patient's phantasy was of destroying the analyst and his wife, and that he (the analyst) would wish to exact a murderous revenge on the patient. The authors convey the analyst's countertransference vividly: he wished to interpret a homosexual transference but had a sense that this would be too comfortable; he felt relief at being able to make light of the nightmare thought but then realised this was an attempt to escape the emotional reality of the situation; finally, there is the curious expression: "the analyst heard himself saying 'The shower is a gas chamber'". Even when the analyst is able to indicate that the current relationship is resonant with the horror of the Holocaust he also disowns the thought – he only "hears himself" say it.

Yet it is clear that progress and something of an emotional breakthrough was achieved in the session. The point at issue, however, is whether, as the authors asserted, the work demonstrated a therapeutic process which was deeper than that provided by a consideration of the transference–countertransference matrix; they claimed that the material examined above was a means of "elucidating the existence of certain psychic processes that *are covered over most of the time by the transference/counter-transference dynamic*" (p. 67, my italics). I have tried to show that, on the contrary, a close examination of the transference–countertransference dynamic reveals that the patient mounted an annihilating attack on his own perception of the analyst and his wife and that the analyst is subliminally aware of this and anxious that, if he were to allow himself to know this more consciously then he would not be able to resist attacking the patient in the way that the living dead do. The clinical situation described by the Botellas is, to my mind, an illustration of the analyst providing a sufficiently safe setting for the patient to approach an appreciation of his murderousness but not sufficiently safe for there to be a fuller exploration of this. The difficulty stems, not from the patient's inability to represent the way his mind functions but rather from the analyst's inability to represent to himself what is happening between him and his patient.

I would like to challenge the view that patients suffer from an inability to represent their greatest fears. In terms of the Sandlers' concept of "understanding work" (1998) it would seem impossible that one could avoid a representation of an event without first of all registering it *and its meaning* albeit in the most rudimentary way.

How could the patient described by the Botellas annihilate/un-represent the analyst and his wife unless he had seen them and then had the hostile impulse to wipe them out? I agree that the processing of the image does not reach the stage at which it can then be repressed, but it must reach a stage in which its meaning is registered sufficiently to warrant annihilation. And it seems to me that the analyst had available his own experience of this: he remembered a pleasant walk with his wife while being confronted with the patient who was severely disturbed by his uncertainty whether he saw his analyst. I would suggest that the analyst himself had to scotomise what he could potentially see because of his fear of his emotional reaction. In that sense, while the murderous hatred could not find representation in patient or analyst, it nevertheless found a register in the transference–countertransference matrix.

I am not totally familiar with the literature which stresses the need of the analyst to regress to the point where they are able to "hallucinate" or "dream" their patient, it otherwise not being possible to find representation of what is happening in the consulting room. I do wonder, however, whether at least some of the reports of this type of approach have arisen because the clinician is unable to register and then represent what is happening for fear of discovering and expressing his own emotional reaction; hence he has to find a more "depersonalised" means of accessing the current reality of the transference and the countertransference. Some accounts of these innovative approaches are open to this reading.

8

HOSTILITY TERMINABLE AND INTERMINABLE

Introduction

In the previous chapter I reviewed some of the clinical work of other schools of psychoanalysis and offered the view that, to a greater or lesser extent, they paid insufficient attention to destructive aggression. One hallmark of the British psychoanalytical tradition in which I was trained and work is an emphasis on the importance of hatred, or hostility, to the other and to the self that requires the presence of the other. This is in contrast to some other schools of psychoanalysis such as those which have put the stress on the analyst being able to think and experience mental states that the patient cannot symbolise. When in 2016 I was involved in an exchange of views with Antonino Ferro, a leading figure in the application of field theory and Bion's later thinking, he confirmed that the patient's destructiveness played little part in his clinical formulations. It was most interesting to find that while we each genuinely respected the other's clinical work we differed on so fundamental a point (PTPP Conference in Wrocław, Poland, October 2016).

I once attended a clinical masterclass at the Tavistock Clinic in which Herbert Rosenfeld was asked why he always tended to concentrate upon and interpret the patient's negative transference and hostility. He replied that he had learnt that if he did not attend to this aspect of the patient's presentation in an interpretation he would at some point enact his hostility to the patient in the way that he spoke. He added that he thought that a part of the patient was as much a victim of a hostile attitude as were the patient's objects. He believed that with such patients it was important to make them aware of the grip that their hostility had upon their functioning and to support them in emancipating themselves from this tyranny. In this sense he did not share Freud's (1937) pessimism about a bedrock of immutability that could not be analysed and which resulted in the impossibility of helping patients emerge from very destructive states of mind. Rosenfeld expanded on these views in his last book where he clarified his belief that there was a sane part of the patient to which the analyst could talk about the way it had been controlled by, or seduced by, or persuaded by, or threatened by, a destructive, narcissistic or even delusional part of the mind (Rosenfeld, 1987, e.g. pp. 111–112).

The huge importance of realising the extent of one's hatred and hostility is indicated by Steiner (2017) in his discussion of some of Klein's unpublished work. He stated that Klein considered love not to be simply an expression of the libido but that it was deepened by depressive anxieties:

> Once we recognize that love is not simply romantic and libidinal, but carries a deep burden of sorrow, guilt, and anxiety, in relation to loved and endangered objects, we can better understand that patients may find love too painful, and will try to avoid and deflect loving feelings, sometimes by increasing hatred and grievance. This means that love is sometimes buried beneath hate, and is only released as the hate is analyzed. We have long understood that hate can be concealed beneath love, but the discovery of loving feelings that have been hidden, is in my view, an important additional understanding that arises if we do not flinch from exploring the deeply painful, and yet enriching complexities of hatred.
>
> (Steiner, 2017; page number not given in referenced text)

The importance of hatred and its handling in a psychoanalytic treatment was also the central thesis in Winnicott's papers on "Hate in the counter-transference" (1949) and "The use of an object" (1969). In the latter paper he described the orientation to external reality that was facilitated by the object being able to survive destructive attacks without retaliating, withdrawing, diminishing receptivity or "crumbling" in some other way (p. 123). Such "crumbling" responses are essentially forms of non-surviving as a concerned, containing object. In the context of an analysis, surviving would involve acknowledging and describing the patient's destructiveness and aggression within a relatively reasoned and dispassionate interpretation: a communication that conveys that the analyst has registered emotionally the fact and extent of the attack and yet can contain his personal reaction and consider the hostility as an important dimension of the clinical situation. In earlier chapters I argued that this was a much more challenging task for the analyst than is sometimes acknowledged but that it is vital if the analysand is to have the experience, in Winnicott's terms, of experiencing an external reality that is in contrast to his projections and his phantasies.

Hopkins (1998) reviewed Winnicott's actual technique with three analytic patients whose treatments are to some extent in the public domain (Harry Guntrip, Masud Khan and Margaret Little). She argued that in each analysis Winnicott avoided a confrontation with the full extent of the patient's destructiveness with severe consequences for the patient's development in the analysis and in their lives after termination of the treatment. Their aggression was fuelled by a destructive narcissism in which pride, grandiosity and a need for control proved more powerful than the ability to accept and receive. Somewhat poignantly given that his analysis had ended and he was about to proceed with the terrible self-destruction that is well documented Hopkins quoted Khan (1969):

> What these patients DEMAND is indulgence and to be adopted, but that is not what they NEED. What they NEED are certain experiences of "a normal nursery" which the repressed aggression and hate of their mothers had made impossible for them. What they NEED is an aggressive encounter and experience in the analytic situation through which they will be able to experience the validity of their own aggression and hate as well as that of the non-self person [the analyst].
>
> (Hopkins, 1998, p. 24, original capitals)

Hopkins described how Winnicott was unable to provide Khan with the experience of encountering his analyst's aggression, including its hateful aspect, and the terrible consequences of this. She also sympathetically noted that Winnicott had a history of heart attacks and was aware of the enormous stress that confronting his own aggression would put on him.

In this chapter I am going to present elements of two analyses with patients for whom hatred and hostility were more ego-syntonic than was love. My aim is to illustrate that the analysis of hatred, while challenging to the analyst, can in some cases be productive and lead to a development of character (first case). The second case demonstrates a failure in such an endeavour, and the possible reasons for this are discussed.

First clinical case: Mr H

Mr H was in his early thirties when he first sought analytic help after moving to the city in the North of England where I have my practice. In the consultation he hinted that he had sought this relocation in order to have an analysis, but when I spoke of this as an indication of his need he aggressively denied it. This was my first taste of his argumentative, occasionally paranoid, character; my attempt to understand it in terms of his difficulty of allowing us to know about his need for help was also denied in a contemptuous way. Nevertheless, he told me that he had heard about psychoanalysis from a friend who had himself had an analysis and had advised him to seek such help after witnessing a furious argument between the patient and a work colleague which had descended into a physical fight. He told me that some people thought he needed anger management treatment, but his colleague had suggested that he needed something deeper than that. When I concurred with this view and said I could see that his way of relating to me was an aspect of his character rather than situational he was initially scathing. However, despite this inauspicious start and somewhat to my surprise, the patient accepted my offer of five times a week analysis in the second consultation session.

He was a slightly built man who moved in a very particular way – it was not quite a swagger but it was intended to convey that he was hard and it would be advisable not to mess with him. His hair was usually cut close to his scalp, and he maintained a hard countenance and a surly combative manner. When he started analysis he had been in a long term relationship with a woman who he claimed not to love but to be "used to"; he said it would not have bothered him had she decided not to move with him. He also told me that he had a long history of conflict with male superiors – this had considerably hampered his professional progress. Despite this he had been reasonably successful in a notoriously competitive and aggressive branch of commerce.

I learned that he was a mountain climber and despised himself for never having climbed in the high Himalayas; his hero was George Mallory who had been "hard" enough and determined enough to attempt Everest twice. The fact that he had died doing so only added to the patient's admiration; he himself often pushed himself beyond his capabilities and belonged to a group of climbers who rejoiced in the bravado of extreme risk. He had once fallen badly while climbing; he had seriously damaged his knee and continuing to climb was often agonisingly painful to him; he prided himself on being able to surmount this physical handicap.

I found it difficult to get a consistent picture of his family. His father had left his mother when the patient was two years old and there was no further contact between them; he never spoke of his father. His mother had re-married when the patient was six – he claimed to get on OK with his step-father but rarely mentioned him. A half-brother was born when the patient was nine but he too very rarely appeared in the patient's material. His principal memories of his childhood and adolescence centred on rows with his mother; each of them would take up very entrenched positions and would accuse the other of being unfair and aggressive; it was then "absolutely vital" not to back down.

His first words in the first session of the analysis were: "This is a crap place – I'm going to hate coming here." An extremely negative transference was quickly established, and many sessions were spent in hostile silence. In the early years of the analysis he always extended analytic breaks by his own absences and could easily slip into a monotonous diatribe in which he accused us both of being useless and "just shit". He seemed to need to be in this state of mind, and I sensed that it reassured him to know that it was always available to him.

I open the front door of the flat where I have my consulting room to my patients and there is a small hallway before the consulting room, which he came to call the "anti-room" (sic). Thus he would say "As soon as I saw you in the anti-room, I didn't want to be here because it's bloody useless and I could see in your face that you felt 'Shit, it's him again.'" At times he seemed actually deluded since he would describe my face as being twisted with hatred. Clearly the forces of hatred and "anti-ness"

162

were released as soon as he saw me and were uncontainable: he felt me to hate him as much as he seemed to hate me. As might be expected there was more than a grain of truth in this since I did not look forward to his sessions and did harbour "anti" feelings against him. Often when I tried to take up his hateful feelings he would feel I was picking on him or "rubbing his nose in his shit" and he would then lapse into a state of hopelessness into which I could be drawn. At other times he would agree with my interpretation but this would only lead to his then masochistically repeating what I had said with a self-hating venom.

However while this useless analysis was going on significant changes were occurring in his external life. Most notably, in the first year of the analysis he occasionally hinted that his partner wanted to have a child but felt hopeless about achieving this. She blamed herself and believed that she was infertile, and he seemed readily to agree that it was all hopeless. As can be imagined I made many interpretations about this, linking it to the transference he had established and his conviction, without undertaking any investigation, that nothing could repair it. Largely I think as a result of this line of interpretation, they did go for a consultation. Medical examination revealed that there were physical complications which were treatable, and eventually his partner gave birth to a daughter. In the immediate aftermath of the birth he expressed his gratitude for the help the analysis had given them but he then began to complain bitterly that his daughter's birth curtailed the possibility of his joining an expedition to climb a really dangerous mountain. He berated himself for not being hard enough or courageous enough to go on this expedition. It was clear how much he resented and was threatened by having received some help which had taken into account his difficulties and hence exposed his vulnerabilities, amongst which was a love for his daughter and a wish that she should not be left fatherless.

Other changes were occurring in the first four years of the analysis although I would only hear about them in passing. He secured an important promotion at work, he married his partner and they bought a house together. However these gains were achieved against a background of seemingly implacable hostility and negativity towards the analysis and me. In the early part of the analysis it often seemed impossible to understand the reasons for his negativity, and it seemed to have a life of its own. For example, the house they bought was in a deprived area and he would frequently complain about all the rubbish that was left in the street. After some analytic work had linked this to the mess he felt he made of the analysis he dreamt that it had all been cleared up; he was in an absolute rage about this "unnecessary and unwanted gentrification and the unnecessary destruction of a working class environment".

At first sight it seemed that he reserved the right to feel rage about all eventualities. However, this dream also helped me understand his fear of losing his aggression and a feeling that without it he would be someone gentrified, tidied up and having lost something that was central to his identity. I now want to present some clinical material that sheds further light on these anxieties. This material is taken from the fourth year of the analysis.

In the sessions leading up to this material I had focused on his attempts to provoke me into interpreting in such a way that he could take my interpretations as criticisms in order to hide his need for analysis and also to assuage his guilt. I thought that this way of thinking had been confirmed when the patient had brought the following dream. He was in some terrible mess that he could not extricate himself from, and his efforts to do so only made things much worse. A colleague was trying to help him, and he felt very grateful for this. His association to this colleague was that he was a man who had his own mind and could "resist the popular mood". He admired this man's ability not to be bullied by group pressures and to stick to his own point of view; he said that this had been helpful to him at work on a number of occasions. I had interpreted that he often tried to get me to express the popular mood which was to be critical of him but when I could resist this, he found it helpful. He appeared moved by this interpretation.

The next day I had to tell him that I would not be able to see him on the Friday of the following week. His immediate reaction had been to wince with pain and to say his knee had just twinged very painfully. A few moments later he said defiantly that he did not want to be subject to the "tyranny" of having to have feelings about my cancellation although he knew that I expected this from patients. He maintained this defiance until the end of the session and mocked my efforts to examine what he felt about my cancellation and to understand why he took this aggressive position – he spoke of my trying to force the "usual analytic interpretations" upon him.

He began the next session by complaining about how dreary my consulting room was. His knee had been very painful; he wished he could find an analgesic that worked. He then told me that he would have to miss his session the following Wednesday and a session later in the month and gave what I felt to be provocatively inadequate reasons for these absences. He went on to describe in some detail various arguments he was involved in at work. He said that of course he expected me to say that all this was further evidence of his destructiveness and obviously he could not disagree with me, because he knew he was provocative and destructive. This was provocative in itself in that any insight and understanding were destructively turned into material for masochistic self-beating.

A little later in that session he told me that he was very ashamed of himself because the previous day he had gone for a walk with his wife and daughter. His daughter had held hands with her mother and he had got very jealous and then offensive. This was also said with some provocation in that he implied he and I were hopeless if we could not stop him behaving like this. I said that he could feel the pain of jealousy and exclusion but that he was quickly searching for an analgesic: he was trying to provoke me into a battle about his cancelling two sessions or about the analysis being hopeless. He was trying to distract us from the fact that he was hurting about the cancelled Friday session and my leaving him to hold someone else's hand: he thought an aggressive confrontation would be the analgesic for this pain. He responded by saying that he had few feelings about me and he doubted whether the cancelled session was important. He then talked about a time when he owned a very fast sports car and could race around the countryside. I suggested that even thinking about feeling excluded or jealous made him feel disempowered and he then quickly put himself into the sports car and that took him right away from his hurt. In response to this he looked sadder and said "Yes".

The next day he seemed depressed in a way that was unusual for him in that it lacked a masochistic edge. Early on in the session he complained that I was such a fool for not realising how he pulled the wool over my eyes, I just didn't realise how awful he was. Yesterday was not a good day. He had arrived at work after his session and there had been a letter containing payment for a report but it was a mistake – it was a colleague who had written the report, so he had had to send the cheque back. Other events

165

had not gone well but the worst thing was that he had met his wife and daughter for a drink at a pub after work. He and his wife had both taken their cars and so there was a question about who the little girl would return home with. She wanted to go with Mummy and his wife saw this upset him and so had said "Why don't you go with Daddy because you've been with me all day." But his daughter insisted on going with her mother and he had got very upset and had driven off aggressively in his car. Later in the evening he had told his daughter that he was not going to read to her in bed. He had also withdrawn from his wife, hadn't wanted to sleep with her, and had thought of leaving home. All of this was told to me with shame but somehow without the usual message that this was further evidence that the analysis was not helping him.

I said that he wanted me to know how ashamed he felt about becoming so angry when he felt rejected and unloved. There was then a long silence in which I increasingly felt that although my interpretation felt more or less right to me it was not making contact with the patient. Remembering what he had said about the letter with the undeserved payment, I said that when he did feel so ashamed and I did not criticise him or try to shame him further but instead tried to understand his vulnerability, he felt I was giving him credit that was not due to him. He emphatically said "Yes and then I think you are a fool!" With more warmth he said that he knew I was not a fool; that after all this time I did know him well. He then said it was time to stop. I said it wasn't but that when he felt understood he wanted to get away because he finds it so hard to feel he deserves anything good. Just before I said it was time to stop the patient said it would be difficult to get off the couch because his knee hurt so badly. As he left he turned and thanked me which was in itself extremely unusual.

Discussion

Denis Carpy (1989) described how the analyst has to struggle to contain the countertransference and that the patient will be aware of this and that this in itself can be "mutative". In this analysis I found that I had to be very aware of my aggressive and combative feelings that were provoked by the patient. Carpy underlined that the countertransference is an unconscious response and that the analyst only became aware of it when he discovers its "conscious derivative" (p. 287). Frequently I only became aware of my aggressive countertransference after I noticed, for example, that my tone or phrasing of an interpretation betrayed my hostility. However this was part of learning to manage the countertransference in order eventually to hold it as a clinical fact and to use it to learn about the patient. In so doing I was observed by the patient, and he could see that I was more able to resist the common mood.

In the manner described by Carpy the patient was able to identify partly with this analytic functioning on my part. Thus, alongside the customary provocation in the material I have reported there was also some capacity for self-observation. He knew he had acted badly with his daughter and wife and he knew this linked to his jealousy and the hurt of exclusion. What he was often unable to do though was to resist turning his observations into an occasion for masochistic self-beating. This was partly out of guilt (he does not deserve any credit) but partly due to another factor that emerged in the following sessions.

Further clinical material

In the Monday session of the following week (in which I would be away on the Friday and he had cancelled the Wednesday session) he spoke of a character in one of his daughter's books who destroyed his own house and tried to live on a rubbish dump as though he did not need a home. However he then reported with some affection a much warmer telephone conversation with his mother. He had then talked about the fractured week in the analysis in such a way that I had interpreted that he wanted to know whether we could meet at another time on Wednesday (the session he had cancelled) without having to ask me directly. He did then ask but could not manage the time I could offer but I could interpret that his analytic home did matter to him. He agreed with this and told me that he had had a good weekend and had felt much closer to his wife and daughter.

He began the Tuesday session by saying that he was worried that he had pressed my door bell longer than usual. He then asked if he could come for the first half an hour of the session I had offered the next day and explained that he had to be at a meeting so would have to leave early. I agreed to this and was not really surprised that there followed a lot of material about arguments, people he would like to kill and the various ways that he was not a nice person at all. Eventually I interpreted that he had got anxious about having asked to come for some of the session tomorrow because it revealed that he was keen on the analysis and I linked this with his anxiety that he had pressed the bell too long. I said I thought he had then wanted to remind us of the vindictive aggressive side of himself as a means of obscuring this more needy, vulnerable and appreciative side.

He said poignantly that he had tried to pretend that my cancelling the Friday session did not matter yet clearly it mattered a lot. Very soon however his tone changed and he called himself "a stupid cunt" for denying that the cancellation mattered. I interpreted that when he did allow himself to feel that he valued and needed the analysis he felt that he was emasculated. He then spoke about seeing a documentary about a man who had been so desperate to become a woman that he had cut off his own penis. The patient had been horrified by this but very moved by the man's desperation. I said he was desperate to allow himself to let go of his "hardness" and "macho-ness" and at the same time it terrified him to be without it. In response he told me that his wife sometimes makes fun of him because when he sees a box of chocolates he becomes like a child – he has to have the ones with soft centres. He said this affectionately and knowingly – I think he was conscious that he was confirming how much he longed to have a soft centre and to be in my soft centre. I found myself moved but time did not allow for the full meaning of this to be explored in that session.

Further discussion

I have described a patient who, for a considerable period of time, found it extremely difficult to allow an interpretation to be experienced as an interpretation. He tended to take my interventions as criticisms which he could then use to masochistically beat himself, with the result that he could then berate both of us for being useless. It is not unusual for patients to allow for the truth of an interpretation but then use it to create an atmosphere in which it cannot be the agent of insight or progress. Any further working through is brought to an abrupt halt because the atmosphere becomes hateful – both sadistic and masochistic. This signals the need, not for abandoning

168

interpretation, but for further analysis of the situation. This almost inevitably involves a period of suffering hopelessness, hatred and despair, and yet, if the setting holds and the analyst continues to try to understand the pressures he and the patient are subject to, then further understanding can emerge. I think my material illustrates this: insight was achieved into why my patient found it so difficult to allow for a softer atmosphere in which his vulnerability and need could be experienced and perceived.

My patient's complex system of defences against anxieties and the way they had become established in creating his character is an illustration of what Steiner (1993) called a "psychic retreat": a pathological stable system of defences against both paranoid and depressive anxieties. In a later contribution (2011) he investigated the forces that militate against an emergence from this kind of pathology. One factor he particularly looked at is the patient's difficulty of allowing themselves to be receptive; in some patients this immediately seems to provoke anxieties about emasculation and of penetration by a phallus. Freud's (1927) understanding of the formation of a fetish focused on the way that the female genitals appeared to confirm the reality of castration. He argued that the fetish is created as a means of substituting an exciting tangible object in the place of a terrifying absence; my patient's excitement and persistence in his aggression suggested that it held a fetishistic fascination for him.

This was a point Freud returned to indirectly in his last but one contribution to clinical psychoanalysis (1937). He wrote there of patients' fear of femininity and he likened the male patient's refusal to submit to a father substitute with the female's refusal to come to terms with a lack of a penis. He wrote that members of both genders can try to "repudiate femininity" and that they can hate the fact that life demands of them an acceptance of painful experience including dependent relationships. Steiner (1993) linked this with the Oedipal situation and the phantasy that its resolution can only occur by a submission to the father's greater power. This did not seem to be the primary cause of the difficulties in Mr A's analysis – his greater anxiety appeared to be his own wish to emasculate himself and allow for a fusion with a maternal object or to be loved by a paternal figure.

In my clinical material there is very little mention of the patient's history, and I have not described any interpretations that attempted to make a re-construction of his childhood. However this is not because I thought his history was not important in forming his

169

character and hence central to the analysis. I could imagine that the means that he and his mother found of coping with the father's disappearance was to deny a sense of loss and to engage in implacable argument where each was hard enough not to give an inch or allow penetration by the other. This would have also protected both of them from the anxiety that, in the absence of the father as a structuring presence, unless they were hard, the needs of their soft centres would lead to some kind of dangerous fusion. For him as a little boy this would have felt very dangerous and would have been linked with castration anxieties and losing his masculine identity. In the last year of his analysis his anxieties about homosexual wishes towards me and the threat to his masculinity were prominent. I came to understand that he had developed defensive identifications which were phallic in nature and could be seen for instance in the way he presented himself physically.

Tuckett (2011) argued that the current emphasis on "here and now" interpretations, "with too little space for formal regression, current expressions of infantile sexual conflicts and other deeper elements of the Freudian unconscious" can result in "psychoanalysis [becoming] a denuded interpersonal psychotherapy" (pp. 1387–1388). I have wanted to show that the analyst's focus on what is the current psychic reality and what this might be a defence against does not necessarily disallow formal regression or for infantile sexual conflicts to be expressed – these very things are expressed and experienced in the present, that is, as Tuckett suggested, they are "current".

In Mr A's case analysis of his character made for substantial development. In fact, his analysis finished when he re-located to further his career in the seventh year of his treatment; had this not happened I think the analysis would have ended naturally only a little later. His relationship with his wife had in the meantime developed further and he could acknowledge the part that his analysis had played in this. Notably his relationship with his mother also noticeably softened; he was much more at ease with her and with people in general.

Second clinical example: Mrs J

An interesting contrast to this essentially successful analysis is provided by Mrs J who was middle-aged when she began a three times a week psychoanalytic therapy. She would only agree to attend three times a week. While this was rationally explained by work commitments which included frequent trips abroad, it also reflected her contempt for the fact that she needed help. The precipitating event which had led her to seek help had been the death of her father. Until his illness they had been almost estranged, but she had visited him in hospital after he had been diagnosed with an untreatable condition. After her father's death she developed neuralgic pain and numbness in her chest and shoulders – this had been extensively investigated and finally diagnosed as being of psychosomatic origin. This was the ostensible reason for seeking help, but she also disclosed that she had been quite manic at times and also, at other times, beside herself with anxiety about her own death.

I discovered that when she had been about five her mother had suffered a severe depressive breakdown and had been hospitalised for many months. She never returned home, and thereafter they only had very sporadic contact with each other. Her father, after his wife's breakdown, began drinking very heavily and having numerous affairs – at this time his business fell apart. The father allowed the family home to become a hippy commune with parties, drugs and promiscuity. This was the setting in which the patient grew up, and she remembers being a thin, unhappy girl who was rebellious at school and who also suffered an extended period of anorexia. At one point she had been befriended by one of her father's friends who showed an interest in her but had then tried to initiate a sexual contact. She emerged from a troubled adolescence with an interest in fashion and she was able to develop this into a business and had achieved very considerable success. She had had no boyfriends in her adolescence and an on-off relationship with a fellow student at college which she told me was a "relationship of convenience"; they had drifted apart in the last year of their course. After a long period of self-enforced abstinence from relationships in her twenties, she met and married a man who came from a stable family and who was able to help her with her difficulty in being close to another person. In her early thirties she had had a daughter, her only child; I gained the impression that she was a committed mother. At times this appeared to be driven by a concern to be seen as doing the right thing, but I was also able to see that there was a genuinely loving side to her relationship with her daughter.

My first impressions on meeting her were of her contempt for herself, for needing to come to see me, and for me as someone who exploited people like her who were in need of help. She later told me that the reason she decided to continue to see me was that in the first meeting I had said that I would need to be prepared to be treated contemptuously. Once we began treatment, she would speak extremely quickly, making it difficult to follow her train of thought with any conviction. Much of the time she seemed intent on ensuring that I had little opportunity to speak and she tried to make sure that I was impressed with her understanding of herself and also her extensive professional successes.

For the first few months I constantly expected her to break off the treatment as she complained that it was unhelpful and certainly not a justifiable use of her valuable time. Although there appeared to me to be regular references to the difficulty she experienced in regard to breaks, attempts on my part to elaborate upon this sensitivity met with scorn and impatience. During a week-long absence in which she had arranged a family holiday she emailed me to say she was ending the therapy forthwith. I received this email late in the evening and I very nearly responded immediately to write back that I thought this was not a good idea and that I hoped to see for her sessions the following week. I decided not to send this email immediately and considered how to respond over the next three days. I eventually emailed her to give almost the same message but I knew that I had treated her communication with respect and had not responded reactively.

When she came to the next session she said that doing so was a defeat. She told me that she had been incredibly anxious about how I would reply to her email and then spoke about her father not noticing that she was neglecting her school work and eating very little. She then told me about dropping her daughter off near her school; the girl had to cross a dual carriageway and had checked to see if it was safe to cross the first carriageway. Having crossed that safely, she had then proceeded at a run to try to cross the second carriageway without checking the traffic. The patient had kept her eye on her daughter, saw a car approaching at speed and had screamed with sufficient alacrity to avoid a tragedy. She accepted my interpretation that she had felt that I had kept a watchful eye on her and had managed to stop her impulsively ending her treatment.

There then followed a period of interesting analytic work in which I was able to feel that the patient, while continuing to be tricky, also showed some interest in understanding herself. For instance, the approach to my consulting room is up some metal stairs, and she told me she made a point of tiptoeing up these so I would not be able to hear her. She was interested in the exploration of the wider meaning of this and could see how it related to her feeling defeated whenever I did manage to comprehend what she was like. She could see how conflicted she was in wanting me to help her and at the same time feeling triumphant if she could thwart me.

I will now report the last session before the first long summer vacation. She began by speaking of a radio report she had heard as she waited in her car for the session. It had been about terminal care for the dying and it reminded her of her father's death and the way that the nurse had gently told her to stop trying to give her father water since he was actually dying. It was only then that she had realised that her father's body was shutting down and his death was imminent; prior to that moment she had denied this.

She then said that her cat had meowed at her that morning; she thought it was hungry but it continued meowing after she had fed it. She followed it into her work room and there was a large dead bird the cat had brought in. It was no use shouting at the cat; it clearly thought it was presenting her with a gift and a triumph: that was its nature. She then said that she had woken up with her left shoulder and whole left side completely numb – she must have "hammered" herself in the night. If anything she was getting worse. I spoke to her about the way that she did have to deny that today we were shutting down – she hammered all awareness and feeling out of herself and moreover she considered it a triumph if she could kill all awareness of my significance to her. She responded thoughtfully and spoke of how she had been left by her mother when she moved out and her father was only interested in parties, drugs and alcohol. She then said dismissively that what she had said was history and what was the point of history? I said the importance of her history was that it was still being lived now. I spoke to her about her current dilemma, she could deny my significance and feel terribly numb and in physical pain, or she could acknowledge that the break was important but she then would feel that I was abandoning her like her parents had done.

She continued to complain about the inadequacies of her father who had made no effort with her; when she had briefly become interested in tennis as a teenager he wouldn't go to the park to play with her; he was only interested in drinking and hated competitive sports. I said she did now have an analyst who was interested in the ways she got into competition and could feel triumphant if she could make me insignificant. She found this initially amusing but when she spoke about how she tried to keep all awareness of problems on my side of the net I thought I could sense a thawing in her attitude.

In the last part of the session she spoke about the man who had befriended her and had groomed her; she had been fortunate that the man had not got violent when she had rejected his advances. I judged that she was here expressing a genuine anxiety, rather than simply accusing me of being an abuser. I said that she did get very anxious when she felt touched by my concern for her and could not, at this moment, distinguish this from an intrusive and sexual advance. At one point I said to her that she now felt as if I was trying physically to touch her and she shuddered and said "Oh, don't"; she conveyed that even my saying this felt viscerally too close. As she left she thanked me, wished me a good break and said she would see me in September.

Discussion

At the beginning of the session Mrs J demonstrated her tendency to attack awareness of a relationship with an object: she would not acknowledge that we are shutting down. She also conveyed, when speaking of her cat, that she regarded this ability to kill off awareness as a part of her nature and as a triumph. However there was some evidence that she could also experience me as the helpful nurse who is informing her of what is happening. Later in the session it became possible to glimpse that as well as seeking to triumph over me she was also desperately defending herself against the enormous anxiety that being touched emotionally created for her: to be touched felt like an assault.

Further material

In the following year of the treatment, while there were convincing indications that Mrs J's relationships with her husband and daughter, together with those people she interacted with professionally, were warmer, I continued to feel that she maintained an emotional distance from me. She steadfastly refused to acknowledge that breaks in the treatment affected her even though at times her material strongly suggested that they caused her considerable disturbance; to allow that this was the case was a complete anathema to her. She would react with increasing hostility to my descriptions of what I took to be communications about her vulnerability to breaks. I found this discrepancy between what she communicated unconsciously in her material including her dreams, and what she maintained to be the truth about herself, that she was immune to loss, difficult to accept and understand. One time as I went to the door to let her into the flat where I work, I suddenly felt a great physical trepidation that when I opened the door I would be confronted by her with a gun in her hand and she would shoot me. Thinking more about this I came to realise that I habitually disregarded, or at least played down, the reality of her hostility, and hence my awareness of it only occasionally broke through to my conscious mind.

In the last session before the long summer break about three years after she had begun the treatment, I interpreted that she was deliberately giving no indication that she was aware that this was our last session for five weeks. She answered pugnaciously that if I was going to assert that the break had any importance whatsoever for her then we might as well stop for good there and then – there would be no point at all in returning. I tried to take up her absolute determination in denying any meaning to the break, and she confirmed that indeed she was so determined.

In the first week following the break it was difficult to gauge quite what her state of mind was. In the first session I heard little of what had happened in the five weeks of the break; instead she tried to engage me in a somewhat academic and argumentative discussion of how I understood her problem. Whatever I said provoked further sceptical or even cynical comments and questions. In the second session she continued in this way but she did say in passing that Ernest had died in the first week of the break. He was a man who was senior in her profession and who had been a very important mentor and support for her early in her career. It had been clear to me before the break that he was someone she respected deeply and felt very attached to, and about whose failing health she had been very worried. Thus I thought it was significant that she had deliberately told me of his

175

death in a casual manner. I pointed this out and she denied that there was any provocative intent in telling me of the death in such a way – it had happened and now it had just happened to come into her mind; she conveyed that I was making a fuss about something which had little meaning for her.

In the third session I was able to say to her that I thought she was playing a cat and mouse or rather cat and bird game with me, deliberately provoking me to speak of her dismissing Ernest's and my importance to her, then dismissing that and waiting for me to try to reach her again. I was surer of my ground and spoke, I felt sure, without the intention of rubbing her nose in what she was doing; I was as sure as one can be in such a situation that I was sympathetically describing to her how she felt compelled to act. She was silent for three or four minutes after I had spoken, which was very unusual, and then said that she had a picture of a mouse sitting in a hole in a piece of cheese: the hole was both its home and its source of sustenance. She associated this to a childhood story she had loved and particularly to the now celebrated relationship between the author and the illustrator of the book. Their working relationship, she said, was deservedly celebrated. She added that she hated the way that some later adaptations of the story had tried to "Americanise" and "Disneyfy" the book and had made it inoffensive and bland.

Taking into account the much softer mood in which she spoke I said that she really appreciated the picture that I had drawn of her, even though it was a picture of her difficulty and her hostility, and of the way that she bites into what can feel like a home and what can sustain her. I added that she preferred that we speak realistically of this rather than adapt to an anodyne version and she appreciated that we could work together to produce this truer picture. She was again quiet for a few moments and then said that what had come into her mind was a memory from the weekend. She had gone into a second-hand bookshop to browse and was annoyed when a mother and her toddler came in because the child was "squally", crying and whingeing. The mother picked up a children's book and forcibly sat the child on her knee and began to read loudly to her son. This had initially annoyed the patient and disturbed her concentration. But after a couple of minutes the little boy became interested in the book and moments later was totally engrossed and then laughing out loud. She told me it was extraordinary; the mother's determination had been "transformative".

176

It was close to the end of the session and I interpreted that she did sense my determination to challenge her squally mood and this too had been transformative – it had transformed her mood from argumentative to one in which she was engrossed by what we were doing together. She did not confirm or deny this but left in a seemingly thoughtful mood.

Later that day I received an email from her with the subject heading of "Thank you". My momentary reaction to seeing this was to be pleasantly surprised, but when I opened the text I read that she was informing me that she had decided, "after much thought", to end the sessions. She wanted to thank me for the help I had given her, it had been invaluable and had made a palpable difference to her life and relationships. She added that she now felt calmer and had been helped to make good decisions during her time with me and that she greatly appreciated this and wished me well. It was clear to me from the tone of her email that she was adamant in her decision and I could see no point in doing anything other than acknowledging that I had received her email and that I understood she had decided to stop. I added that to my mind this was not a good decision; I understood I had to accept it and that should she in the future decide to take up therapy again then I would be happy to talk to her about this. She responded briefly, thanking me.

Discussion

I was left to ponder what had happened in that last session and in the therapy as a whole. I was in no doubt that Mrs J had dropped her hostile and provocative stance towards the latter part of the session and had revealed a genuine and moving appreciation of our work together. It seemed that when she realised this it became imperative to end her treatment. Could I have done something to avoid this? Would there have been a different outcome if there had been time to interpret that our good collaboration, which she valued, would be ambushed by her telling herself that my aim was to "Disneyfy" her and that she would find it hard to resist a certainty about this? Was there some truth in her possible view that I was scotomising her hostility and not seeing it for the deadly force she felt it to be. Certainly my initial reaction to seeing her email headlined "Thank you", which was to be surprised that she was taking the trouble to thank me for a helpful session, suggests a naivety on my part. It indicates that I had not paid sufficient heed to her warning before the break that if I continued to suggest that her sessions were important to her then we should stop "there and then". While she acknowledged that she was grateful for what we had achieved, which I think was genuine, she nevertheless must have reacted violently to the experience of having a parent who could transform her by getting hold of her and helping her to understand her story and herself. With hindsight I could see that my imagining that she would shoot me when I opened the door to her was an indication that I was sensitive to her murderous hostility but I think I failed to grasp this sufficiently. Had I done so, I might have been in a better position to describe to her the power that her hostility commanded and the helplessness that she felt in confronting it and standing up to it.

General discussion

In "Analysis terminable and interminable" (1937) Freud argued that the prognosis for an illness treated by psychoanalysis was much more favourable if the pathology was a product of trauma rather than constitutional factors. He recognised that the aetiology in almost every case was mixed, but:

> The stronger the constitutional factor, the more readily will a trauma lead to a fixation and leave behind a developmental disturbance; the stronger the trauma, the more certainly will its injurious effects become manifest even when the instinctual situation is normal. There is no doubt that an aetiology of the traumatic sort offers by far the more favourable field for analysis. ... Only when a case is a predominantly traumatic one will analysis succeed in doing what it is so superbly able to do so; only then will it, thanks to having strengthened the patient's ego, succeed in replacing by a correct solution the inadequate decision made in his early life.
>
> (p. 220)

And:

> If we ask what is the source of the great variety of kinds and degrees of alteration of the ego, we cannot escape the first

178

obvious alternative, that such alterations are either congenital or acquired. Of these, the second sort will be the easier to treat.

(p. 235)

It might be possible to argue that Mrs J's hostility had a greater constitutional basis than had Mr H's; certainly the material about her cat suggests a constitutional or "natural" source for her hostility, but this would be an essentially tautological explanation. Both patients had traumatic backgrounds with the loss of important figures and the inability of others to adapt in order to compensate in some way for the losses. Mr H's hostility was much more upfront and pervaded his manner and appearance in a way that Mrs J's did not. Prior to coming into treatment she seemed to have made greater progress in adapting her life to take into account and limit her hostility: she had married, valued the stability her husband provided, was a good mother and had made exceptional professional progress. Mr H, in contrast had a contentious relationship, his professional life had been marred by his aggressive outbursts and he had deliberately endangered his life. On that basis one might think that Mrs J's difficulties would be more amenable to treatment and have a more traumatic, rather than constitutional, origin. And yet it was Mr H who was able to make better use of his analysis and to allow his treatment to "strengthen" his ego i.e. to develop a greater tolerance of himself and his needs and vulnerabilities. Undoubtedly he was able to love more profoundly once his hostility was better understood and his depressive anxieties deepened his capacity for concern. While at first sight his hostility seemed more ego-syntonic than did Mrs J's, in fact analysis revealed that it was to a large extent intended to protect him from his underlying wish for a loving relationship with all the vulnerability that came with that.

One reason I was able to keep a more constant awareness of Mr H's hostility was that it was much more upfront than was Mrs J's. I consider it was a failure on my part not to sufficiently register the depth of her hostility and in this way I committed the same clinical mistake that Hopkins described in Winnicott's analysis of Khan and others. While Mr H was enabled to suffer his distress and in effect eventually aligned himself with Tennyson's view that it is better to have loved and lost then never to have loved at all, in Mrs J this possibility excited her killer instinct which she could not then resist.

179

In her paper on Winnicott's analysis of Khan, Hopkins (1998) posed the question of why the treatment did not help Khan have better control of his destiny. She wondered whether he might have been "one of those patients who just can't be helped". Without having dismissed that possibility, Hopkins pointed to weaknesses in the personalities of both protagonists "as well as other contributing factors, that went beyond the inevitable limitations of analysis". The weaknesses she described were too great a timidity on the part of the analyst and too great a hostility to his own need for help on the part of the patient. In Mrs J's case it was principally my failure, actually similar to that of Winnicott's, to take full account of her hostility that I hold responsible for the premature ending of the treatment. Had I been able to keep in mind that she would always be tempted to kill off the analysis I might have been better able to describe this to her and thus help her to struggle more effectively against her nature. While I am aware that different views can be advanced for the sudden termination of this analysis and my responsibility for this I believe that a fundamental failing was due to my blind spot and my insufficient regard of her hostility. This conclusion parallels the experience of Freud who in 1914 championed the outbreak of war since he considered it "a chivalrous passage of arms" (Schimmel, 2018). It was only as he became aware of the reality of war that he lamented his earlier enthusiasm in a letter to Lou Andreas-Salomé: "And the saddest thing about it is that it is exactly the way we should have expected people to behave from our knowledge of psychoanalysis" (Pfeiffer, 1963, p. 21).

References

Arlow, J.A. (1963). The supervisory situation. *J. Am. Psychoanal. Assn.*, 11:576–594.

Bader, M.J. (1994). The tendency to neglect therapeutic aims in psychoanalysis. *Psychoanal. Q.*, 63:246–270.

Baranger, M. and Baranger, W. (2008). The analytic situation as a dynamic field. *Int. J. Psycho-Anal.*, 89:795–826.

Baranger, M., Baranger, W. and Mom, J. (1983). Process and non-process in analytic work. *Int. J. Psycho-Anal.*, 64:1–15.

Bazan, A. (2017). Alpha synchronization as a brain model for unconscious defence: an overview of the work of Howard Shevrin and his team. *Int. J. Psychoanal.*, 98:1443–1473.

Bell, D. (2015). The death drive: phenomenological perspectives in contemporary Kleinian theory. *Int. J. Psychoanal.*, 96:411–423.

Benjamin, J. (2009a). A relational psychoanalysis perspective on the necessity of acknowledging failure in order to restore the facilitating and containing features of the intersubjective relationship (the shared third). *Int. J. Psychoanal.*, 90:441–450.

Benjamin, J. (2009b). Response. *Int. J. Psychoanal.*, 90:457–462.

Berman, E. (2000). Psychoanalytic supervision. *Int. J. Psychoanal.*, 81 (2):273–290.

Bernardi, R. (2008). Letter from Uruguay. *Int. J. Psychoanal.*, 89(2):233–240.

Bernardi, R. (2011). The challenge to and of the "outsider": the reception of Kohut's ideas by an analyst trained in a different tradition. *Psychoanal. Inq.*, 31(5):448–461.

Bion, W.R. (1959). Attacks on linking. *Int. J. Psycho-Anal.*, 40:308–315.

Bion, W.R. (1962). *Learning from experience*. London: Tavistock.

Bion, W.R. (1965). *Transformations: change from learning to growth*. London: Tavistock.

Bion, W.R. (1970). *Attention and interpretation*. London: Tavistock.

Bion, W.R. (2005). *The Italian seminars*. London: Karnac.

Birksted-Breen, D. (2009). "Reverberation time", dreaming and the capacity to dream. *Int. J. Psychoanal.*, 90:35–51.

Birksted-Breen, D. (2010). Is translation possible? *Int. J. Psychoanal.*, 91 (4):687–694.

Birksted-Breen, D. (2012). Taking time: the tempo of psychoanalysis. *Int. J. Psychoanal.*, 93(4):819–835.

Birksted-Breen, D. (2016). Bi-ocularity, the functioning mind of the psychoanalyst. *Int. J. Psychoanal.*, 97:25–40.

Blass, R.B. (2009). An introduction. *Int. J. Psychoanal.*, 90(3):437–439.

Blass, R. (2010a). On: the comments of Emanuel Berman, Lewis Aron, Yoram Hazan and Steven Stern. *Int. J. Psychoanal.*, 91(5):1285–1287.

Blass, R.B. (2010b). Affirming "that's not psycho-analysis!": on the value of the politically incorrect act of attempting to define the limits of our field. *Int. J. Psychoanal.*, 91:81–99.

Blum, H.P. (1974). The borderline childhood of the Wolf Man. *J. Am. Psychoanal. Assn.*, 22:721–742.

Botella, C. and Botella, S. (2005). *The work of psychic figurability: mental states without representation.* Trans. A. Weller. Hove: Brunner-Routledge.

Brandchaft, B., Doctors, S. and Sorter, D. (2010). *Towards an emancipatory psychoanalysis.* New York: Routledge.

Brenman, E. (2006). *Recovery of the lost good object.* London: Routledge.

Brenman Pick, I. (1985). Working through in the countertransference. *Int. J. Psycho-Anal.*, 66:157–166.

Brenman Pick, I. (2012). Working through in the countertransference: second thoughts. Paper given to a Scientific Meeting of the BPAS.

Brenner, C. (1982). The concept of the superego: a reformulation. *Psychoanal Q.*, 51:501–525.

Britton, R. (2003). *Sex, death and the superego.* London: Karnac.

Caligor, L. (1981). Parallel and reciprocal processes in psychoanalytic supervision. *Contemp. Psychoanal.*, 17:1–27.

Caper, R. (1992). Does psychoanalysis heal? A contribution to the theory of psychoanalytic technique. *Int. J. Psycho-Anal.*, 73:283–292.

Caper, R. (1999). *A mind of one's own: a Kleinian view of self and object.* London: Routledge.

Carpy, D.V. (1989). Tolerating the countertransference: a mutative process. *Int. J. Psycho-Anal.*, 70:287–294.

Chasseguet-Smirgel, J. (1985). *The ego ideal: a psychoanalytic essay on the malady of the ideal.* Trans. P. Barrows. London: Free Association Books.

Collins, S. (1980). Freud and "the riddle of suggestion". *Int. Rev. Psycho-Anal.*, 7:429–437.

Cooper, A.M. (1986). Some limitations on therapeutic effectiveness: the "burnout syndrome" in psychoanalysts. *Psychoanal. Q.*, 55:576–598.

Cooper, A.M. (2008). Commentary on Greenson's "The working alliance and the transference neurosis". *Psychoanal. Q.*, 77(1):103–119.

De M'Uzan, M. (1976). Countertransference and the paradoxical system. In: De M'Uzan, M. (ed.). *Death and identity: being and the psycho-sexual drama*, pp. 17–32. Trans. A. Weller. London: Karnac, 2013.

Doehrman, M. (1976). Parallel process in supervision and psychotherapy. *Bull. Mennin. Clinic.*, 40:3–104.

Eissler, K.S. (1953). The effect of the structure of the ego on psychoanalytic technique. *J. Amer. Psychoanal. Assn.*, 1:104–143.

Fajrajzen, S. (2014). The compulsion to confess and the compulsion to judge in the analytic situation. *Int. J. Psychoanal.*, 95:977–933.

Feldman, M. (1997). Projective identification: the analyst's involvement. *Int. J. Psycho-Anal.*, 78:227–241.

Ferro, A. (2009). Transformations in dreaming and characters in the psychoanalytic field. *Int. J. Psychoanal.*, 90:209–230.

Frank, C. (2015). On the reception of the concept of the death drive in Germany: expressing and resisting an "evil principle". *Int. J. Psychoanal.*, 96:425–444.

Freud, S. (1893). The psychotherapy of hysteria from *Studies on hysteria. S. E.*, II:253–305.

Freud, S. (1898). Letter from Freud to Fliess, 26 August 1898. In Masson, J.M. (ed.). *The complete letters of Sigmund Freud to Wilhelm Fliess, 1887–1904*. London: Belknap Press, 1985.

Freud, S. (1905). *Fragments of an analysis of a case of hysteria. S.E.*, VII:1–122.

Freud, S. (1906). Psychoanalysis and the establishment of the facts in legal proceedings. *S.E.*, IX:97–114.

Freud, S. (1909). *Analysis of a phobia in a five-year-old boy* ("Little Hans"). *S. E.*, X:5–147.

Freud, S. (1910a). Letter from Sándor Ferenczi to Sigmund Freud, 13 February 1910. In: Brabant, E. et al. (eds.). *The correspondence of Sigmund Freud and Sándor Ferenczi: Volume 1, 1908–1914*, pp. 136–139. London: Belknap Press, 1993.

Freud, S. (1910b). The future prospects of psycho-analytic therapy. *S.E.*, XI:139–151.

Freud, S. (1912). Recommendations to physicians practising psycho-analysis. *S.E.*, XI:109–120.

Freud, S. (1913). The disposition to obsessional neurosis. *S.E.*, XII:311–326.

Freud, S. (1914a). Remembering, repeating and working-through. (Further recommendations on the technique of psycho-analysis II). *S.E.*, XII:145–156.

Freud, S. (1914b). On the history of the psycho-analytic movement. *S.E.*, XIV:1–66.

Freud, S. (1914c). *On narcissism. S.E.*, XIV:67–102.

Freud, S. (1915a). Instincts and their vicissitudes. *S.E.*, XIV:109–140.

Freud, S. (1915b). The unconscious. *S.E.*, XIV:159–215.

Freud, S. (1916). *Introductory lectures on psycho-analysis. S.E.*, XV:1–240.

Freud, S. (1917a). Mourning and melancholia. *S.E.*, XIV:237–260.

Freud, S. (1917b). *Introductory lectures on psycho-analysis* (part three). *S.E.*, XV:241–463.

Freud, S. (1918). *From the history of a childhood neurosis. S.E.*, XVII:3–123.

Freud, S. (1919). The "uncanny". *S.E.*, XVII:219–256.

Freud, S. (1920). *Beyond the pleasure principle. S.E.*, XVIII:1–64.

Freud, S. (1921). *Group psychology and the analysis of the ego. S.E.*, XVIII:65–144.

Freud, S. (1923). *The ego and the id. S.E.*, XIX:1–66.

Freud, S. (1927). Fetishism. *S.E.*, XXI:149–157.

Freud, S. (1930). *Civilization and its discontents. S.E.*, 21:57–146.

Freud, S. (1933a). *New introductory lectures on psycho-analysis. S.E.*, XXII:1–182.

Freud, S. (1933b). Sándor Ferenczi. *S.E.*, XXII:225–230.

Freud, S. (1937). Analysis terminable and interminable. *S.E.*, XXIII:209–254.

Freud, S. (1938). *An outline of psychoanalysis. S.E.*, XXIII:139–208.

Freud, S. (1939). *Moses and monotheism. S.E.*, 23:1–138.

Gabbard, G.O. (2007). "Bound in a nutshell": thoughts on complexity, reductionism, and "infinite space". *Int. J. Psychoanal.*, 88:559–574.

Gardiner, M.M. (1983). The Wolf Man's last years. *J. Am. Psychoanal. Assn.*, 31:867–897.

Gay, P. (1988). *A life for our time.* New York: Norton.

Gray, P. (1987). On the technique of analysis of the superego: an introduction. *Psychoanal. Q.*, 56:130–154.

Greenson, R.R. (1965). The working alliance and the transference neurosis. *Psychoanal. Q.*, 34:155–181.

Grotstein, J.S. (2004). Notes on the superego. *Psychoanal. Inq.*, 24:257–270.

Hartmann, H. and Kris, E. (1945). The genetic approach in psychoanalysis. *Psychoanal. St. Child*, 1:11–30.

Hartmann, H., Kris, E. and Loewenstein, R.M. (1946). Comments on the formation of psychic structure. *Psychoanal. St. Child*, 2:11–38.

Heimann, P. (1950). On countertransference. *Int. J. Psycho-Anal.*, 31:81–84.

Hopkins, L.B. (1998). D. W. Winnicott's analysis of Masud Khan: a preliminary study of failures of object usage. *Contemp. Psychoanal.*, 34 (1):5–47.

Ingham, G. (2007). The superego, narcissism and great expectations. *Int. J. Psychoanal.*, 88:753–768.

International Psychoanalytical Association. (2018). Draft report of the IPA Confidentiality Committee. (16 April).

Ithier, B. (2016). The arms of the chimeras. *Int. J. Psychoanal.*, 97(2):451–478.

Jacobs, D. (2016). Review of *Clinical supervision of psychoanalytical psychotherapy*. Ed. Scharff, J. (2014). *J. Am. Psychoanal. Assn.*, 64:431–437.

Jacobson, E. (1946). The effect of disappointment on ego and super-ego formation in normal and depressive development. *Psychoanal. Rev.*, 33:129–147.

Jacobson, E. (1954). On psychotic identifications. *Int. J. Psycho-Anal.*, 35:102–108.

Joseph, B. (1989). *Psychic equilibrium and psychic change: selected papers of Betty Joseph*. Feldman, M. and Spillius, E.B. (eds.). New library of psycho-analysis. London: Routledge.

Kantrowitz, J.L. (2004). Writing about patients. *J. Am. Psychoanal. Assn.*, 52(1):69–99.

Keats, J. (1817). Letter to George and Thomas Keats, 21 December 1817. In: Hunter, J.P. (ed.). *The Norton introduction to literature: poetry*. New York: W.W. Norton, 1973.

Kernberg, O.F. (1974). Further contributions to the treatment of narcissistic personalities. *Int. J. Psycho-Anal.*, 55:215–240.

Khan, M.M.R. (1969). Vicissitudes of being, knowing and experiencing in the therapeutic situation. In: Khan, M.M.R. (ed.). *The privacy of the self*, pp. 203–218. Madison, CT: International Universities Press, 1974.

Klein, M. (1948). A contribution to the theory of anxiety and guilt. *Int. J. Psycho-Anal.*, 29:114–123.

Klein, M. (1958). On the development of mental functioning. In: Klein, M. (ed.). *Envy and gratitude and other works, 1946–1963*, pp. 236–246. London: Hogarth Press, 1975.

Kohut, H. (1979). The two analyses of Mr Z. *Int. J. Psycho-Anal.*, 60:3–27.

Kohut, H. (1984). *How does analysis cure?* Goldberg, A. and Stepansky, P. (eds.). Chicago: University of Chicago Press.

Kramer, P. (1958). Note on one of the pre-Oedipal roots of the superego. *J. Am. Psychanal. Assoc.*, 6:38–46.

Langer, M. (1962). Symposium: selection criteria for the training of psycho-analytic students. *Int. J. Psycho-Anal.*, 43:272–276.

Laplanche, J. and Pontalis, J.B. (1973). *The language of psycho-analysis*. London: Hogarth Press and the Institute of Psycho-Analysis.

Loewald, H. (1960). On the therapeutic action of psychoanalysis. In: Loewald, H. (ed.). *Papers on psychoanalysis*, pp. 221–256. New Haven, CT: Yale University Press, 1980.

Malcolm, R.R. (1988). The constitution and operation of the super ego. *Psychoanal. Psychother.*, 3:149–159.

Meissner, W.W. (1977). The Wolf Man and the paranoid process. *Annu. Psychoanal.*, 5:23–74.

Milton, J. (1994). Abuser and abused: perverse solutions following childhood abuse. *Psychoanal. Psychother.*, 8(3):243–255.

Mollon, P. (1993). *The fragile self.* London: Wiley.

Money-Kyrle, R.E. (1956). Normal counter-transference and some of its deviations. *Int. J. Psycho-Anal.*, 37:360–366.

Money-Kyrle, R.E. (1968). Cognitive development. *Int. J. Psycho-Anal.*, 49:691–698.

Money-Kyrle, R. (1971). The aim of psychoanalysis. *Int. J. Psycho-Anal.*, 52:103–106.

Ogden, T. (1994). The analytic third: working with intersubjective clinical facts. *Int. J. Psycho-Anal.*, 75:3–19.

O'Shaughnessy, E. (1975). Explanatory notes. In: Klein, M. (ed.). *Envy and gratitude and other works, 1946–1963*, pp. 324–336. London: Hogarth Press.

O'Shaughnessy, E. (1999). Relating to the superego. *Int. J. Psychoanal.*, 80:861–870.

Perelberg, R.H. (2015). On excess, trauma and helplessness: repetitions and transformations. *Int. J. Psychoanal.*, 96:1453–1476.

Pfeiffer, E. (ed). (1963). *Sigmund Freud and Lou Andreas-Salomé: letters.* London: Hogarth Press and the Institute of Psychoanalysis.

Poland, W.S. (1975). Tact as a psychoanalytic function. *Int. J. Psycho-Anal.*, 56:155–162.

Poland, W.S. (2002). The interpretive attitude. *J. Am. Psychoanal. Assn.*, 50(3):807–826.

Poland, W.S. (2009). Problems of collegial learning in psychoanalysis: narcissism and curiosity. *Int. J. Psychoanal.*, 90:249–262.

Quinodoz, J. (2010). How translations of Freud's writings have influenced French psychoanalytic thinking. *Int. J. Psychoanal.*, 91(4):695–716.

Rangell, L. (2008). Reconciliation: the continuing role of theory. *J. Am. Acad. Psychoanal. Dyn. Psychiatr.*, 36(2):217–233.

Reich, A. (1954). Early identifications as archaic elements in the superego. *J. Am. Psychoanal. Assn.*, 2:218–238.

Reich, A. (1960). Pathologic forms of self-esteem regulation. *Psychoanal. St. Child*, 15:215–232.

Roazen, P. (1979). *Freud and his followers.* London: Peregrine.

Rocha Barros, E.D. and Lieberman, J.S. (2000). The search for meaning in the affective expressions of the adolescent patient. *Int. J. Psychoanal.*, 81(2):324–327.

Rosenfeld, H. (1971). A clinical approach to the psychoanalytic theory of the life and death instincts: an investigation into the aggressive aspects of narcissism. *Int. J. Psycho-Anal.*, 52:169–178.

Rosenfeld, H. (1987). *Impasse and interpretation.* London: Tavistock.

Sandler, J. (1960). On the concept of the superego. *Psychoanal. St. Child*, 15:128–162.

Sandler, J., Holder, A. and Meers, D. (1963). The ego ideal and the ideal self. *Psychoanal. St. Child*, 18:139.

Sandler, J. and Sandler, A. (1984). The past unconscious, the present unconscious, and interpretation of the transference. *Psychoanal. Inq.*, 4 (3):367–399.

Sandler, J. and Sandler, A.M. (1987). The past unconscious, the present unconscious and the vicissitudes of guilt. *Int. J. Psycho-Anal.*, 68:331–341.

Sandler, J. and Sandler, A.-M. (1998). *Internal objects revisited*. London: Karnac.

Schafer, R. (1960). The loving and beloved superego in Freud's structural theory. *Psychoanal. St. Child*, 15:163–188.

Schimmel, P. (2018). Freud's "selected fact": his journey of mourning. *Int. J. Psychoanal.*, 99:208–229.

Searles, H. (1955). The informational value of the supervisor's emotional experiences. *Psychiatry*, 18:135–146.

Sedlak, V. (1997). The dream space and countertransference. *Int. J. Psycho-Anal.*, 78:295–305.

Sedlak, V. (2003). The patient's material as an aid to the disciplined working through of the countertransference and supervision. *Int. J. Psychoanal.*, 84:1487–1500.

Sedlak, V. (2009). Discussion. *Int. J. Psychoanal.*, 90:451–455.

Sedlak, V. (2016). The psychoanalyst's normal and pathological superegos. *Int. J. Psychoanal.*, 97:1499–1152.

Segal, H. (1991). *Dream phantasy and art*. New library of psychoanalysis. London: Routledge.

Segal, H. (1993). On the clinical usefulness of the concept of the death instinct. *Int. J. Psycho-Anal.*, 74:55–61.

Sharpe, E. (1950). The technique of psycho-analysis. In: Sharpe, E. (ed.). *Collected papers on psycho-analysis*, pp. 9–21. London: Hogarth Press.

Sklar, J. (2012). Regression and new beginnings: Michael, Alice and Enid Balint and the circulation of ideas. *Int. J. Psychoanal.*, 93(4):1017–1034.

Smith, H.F. (2003). Can we integrate the diverse theories and practices of psychoanalysis? *J. Am. Psychoanal. Assn.*, 51S(Supplement):127–144.

Solomon, R.Z. (1992). The psychoanalytic core. Essays in honor of Leo Rangell, M.D.: edited by Harold P. Blum, M.D., Edward M. Weinshel, M.D., and F. Robert Rodman, M.D. Madison, CT: International Universities Press, Inc., 1989. 536 pp. *Psychoanal Q.*, 61:449–453.

Spence, D.P. (1997). Case reports and the reality they represent: the many faces of *Nachträglichkeit*. In: Ward, I. (ed.). *The presentation of case material in clinical discourse*, pp. 77–94. London: Freud Museum.

Spillius, E.B. (1994). Developments in Kleinian thought: overview and personal view. *Psychoanal. Inq.*, 14:324–364.

Steiner, J. (1993). *Psychic retreats*. London: Routledge.

Steiner, J. (2011). *Seeing and being seen*. London: Routledge.

Steiner, J. (2013). Reflections on the work of Hanna Segal. Paper presented at the Hanna Segal Memorial Conference, London, May 2013.

Steiner, J. (2017). Melanie Klein's technique then and now. *Inst Psa UK AV Proj Videostream*, 1(1):15 (accessed via www.pep-web.org).

Stolorow, R.D. (1975). Toward a functional definition of narcissism. *Int. J. Psycho-Anal.*, 56:179–185.

Strachey, J. (1934). The nature of the therapeutic action of psycho-analysis. *Int. J. Psycho-Anal.*, 15:127–159.

Symington, N. (2007). A technique for facilitating change in the creation of mind. *Int. J. Psychoanal.*, 88:1409–1422.

Taylor, D. (2011). Commentary on Vermote's "On the value of 'late Bion' to analytic theory and practice". *Int. J. Psychoanal.*, 92:1099–1112.

Tuckett, D. (2011). Inside and outside the window: some fundamental elements in the theory of psychoanalytical technique. *Int. J. Psychoanal.*, 92:1367–1390.

Tuckett, D., Basile, R., Birksted-Breen, D., Bohm, T., Denis, P., Ferro, A., Hinz, H., Jemstedt, A., Mariotti, P. and Schubert, J. (2008). *Psychoanalysis comparable and incomparable: the evolution of a method to describe and compare psychoanalytic approaches*. London: Routledge.

Vermote, R. (2011). On the value of "late Bion" to analytic theory and practice. *Int. J. Psychoanal.*, 92:1089–1098.

Waelder, R. (1962). Psychoanalysis, scientific method, and philosophy. *J. Am. Psychoanal. Assn.*, 10:617–637.

Wallerstein, R.S. (1988). One psychoanalysis or many? *Int. J. Psycho-Anal.*, 69:5–21.

Wallerstein, R.S. (1990). Psychoanalysis: the common ground. *Int. J. Psycho-Anal.*, 71:3–20.

Ward, I. (ed.). (1997). *The presentation of case material in clinical discourse*. London: Freud Museum.

Widlöcher, D. (1978). The ego ideal of the psychoanalyst. *Int. J. Psycho-Anal.*, 59:387–390.

Widlöcher, D. (2002). Presidential address. *Int. J. Psychoanal.*, 83(1):205–210.

Winnicott, D.W. (1949). Hate in the counter-transference. *Int. J. Psycho-Anal.*, 30:69–74.

Winnicott, D.W. (1965). A clinical study of the effect of a failure of the average expectable environment on a child's mental functioning. *Int. J. Psycho-Anal.*, 46:81–87.

Winnicott, D.W. (1969). The use of an object. *Int. J. Psycho-Anal.*, 50:711–716.

Index

abuse 74, 117–118
affective pictograms 153
ageing 18, 19, 22
aggrandisement 34
aggression: analysts' aggressive
 reaction 27, 70; death instinct
 37; as drive 36; healthy versus
 hostile/destructive 3; and
 hostility 160; Mr A 16; Mr G
 105; Mr H 162, 168, 169, 179;
 self psychology 145, 147; and
 the superego 34, 35, 38, 42
alpha functions 28
ambivalent relationship 45
analytic third 151
anger 25, 27; *see also* rage
annihilation 37, 156, 157
anti-therapeutic factors 91
anxiety: analysts' 106, 107, 109,
 122, 124, 125–126, 131;
 anxiety-dread continuum 54–55,
 65; archaic anxiety 55;
 communication about 120; and
 sadism 80
archaic objects 45, 47
Arlow, J.A. 116–117, 128
assessment for psychoanalysis 94
authoritarian figures 33, 35

bad objects 45, 141–142, 144
Bader, M.J. 78
Baranger, M. 152
Baranger, W. 152
Bazan, A. 116
Bell, D. 37
Benjamin, Jessica 137–142, 146
Berman, E. 113, 121
Bernardi, R. 133, 148
beta elements 28, 29–30
Bion, Wilfred 10, 13, 28, 29–30,
 37, 55, 63–64, 66–67, 69, 77,
 82, 84, 152, 158
Birksted-Breen, D. 131, 132,
 151–152
birth 37–38
Blass, R.B. 131, 137
boredom, analysts' 24, 26, 28,
 99–100
Botella, César 150–151, 153,
 156–157
Botella, Sára 150–151, 153,
 156–157
boundaries, crossing 27
Brandchaft, B. 137, 142, 146–147
breakdowns 19, 24, 57–58, 62, 93,
 117, 171
breast 13, 38, 39, 66, 143

189

self psychology 144, 147, 148; and the superego 37, 38, 40; as unhealthy aggression 3–4
developmental trajectories of the ego ideal 80–84
developmental trajectories of the superego 41–42
Dickens, Charles 42
disappointment 85
disavowal 12
discomfort 5, 21, 25, 28, 30, 86
dissociation 140
Doehrman, M. 127
Dora 116
double, concept of the 153–154
doubt, entertaining realistic 92
dread 53–68
dreams: analysts' 27; importance of dream space and dreaming 29; and intuition 152, 153, 154, 157; as latent unconscious knowledge 115; Mr A 14–15; Mr B 21, 22; Mr C 24, 25, 26; Mr H 164; Mrs D 60, 62; Mrs F 95–96, 98–99; nightmares 21, 22, 26, 118, 154–155, 156; supervision one case 118–119, 120
drive, as healthy aggression 3
drives 36, 37, 144

ego, and the superego 35–36, 39, 40, 41, 128
ego ideals 69–88; analysts' 73–81, 84–87, 130; concept of 70–87; depressive/reparative ego ideal 70, 78–81, 131; development of professional 81–84; Freud used interchangeably with superego

33; parental ego ideal 70, 76; and supervision 127
ego psychology 32, 33–35
Eissler, K.S. 78
enactment 28, 50, 105, 127, 139
ending the therapeutic relationship 57, 103–104, 124, 126, 137, 172, 173, 177, 180
envy 3, 66, 67
epistemological warfare 131
Eros and Thanatos 5
ethics committees 57, 59
European Psychoanalytic Federation 148
evidence base 132–133
experience-near concepts 90

failed analysis 54, 89–110, 131, 135, 170–178
Fajrajzen, S. 12, 62, 66, 82, 146
fantasies 50–51, 120, 151
fathers: Mr A 14–15, 16–17; Mr B 19; Mr C 24; Mr H 162, 170; Mrs F 97; Mrs J 171, 172, 173, 174; and the Oedipus complex 33; Sandman 65; and the superego 34, 35; supervision one case 117; Wolf Man 135
fear 46–47, 55, 65, 70, 74, 77, 96, 156
Feldman, M. 73–74
Ferenczi, Sandor 77, 133, 135
Ferro, Antonio 152, 153, 158
fetishes 169
field theory 158
figurability 153–154, 155
Frank, C. 36, 37
free associations 69, 151
Freud, Sigmund: anxiety 55; conquistador of new knowledge

trauma 62, 144, 178, 179
trustworthiness 74, 75, 76
truth 31, 68, 70, 137, 144
Tuckett, D. 74–75, 149, 170

uncanniness 65
uncertainty, tolerating 28
unconscious: analysts' 3;
   communication 116; dream
   work 153; expressions of
   analysts' pathological superego
   48; moral judgement 150;
   patients' 3; patients
   unconsciously pitch material
   beyond extent of analysts'
   understanding 18; present
   unconscious 142; subtle
   enactments of analyst's 50; and
   the superego 32, 40; surface
   expressions of 115–116

understanding work 115–116, 127,
   128, 156

Vermote, R. 152, 153
Vienna 112–113
visual images 151–152, 176

Waelder, R. 132
waiting rooms 27
Wallerstein, R.S. 142, 143,
   144, 148
Ward, I. 132
Widlöcher, D. 75–76, 87, 88, 133
Winnicott, Donald 55, 94, 159,
   160, 179–180
withholding 19
Wolf Man 133–137
working alliance 78

Ziehen, Theodor 134

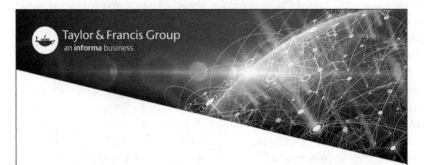